Giotto and His Works in Padua

David Zwirner Books

ekphrasis

Giotto and His Works in Padua

John Ruskin

Contents

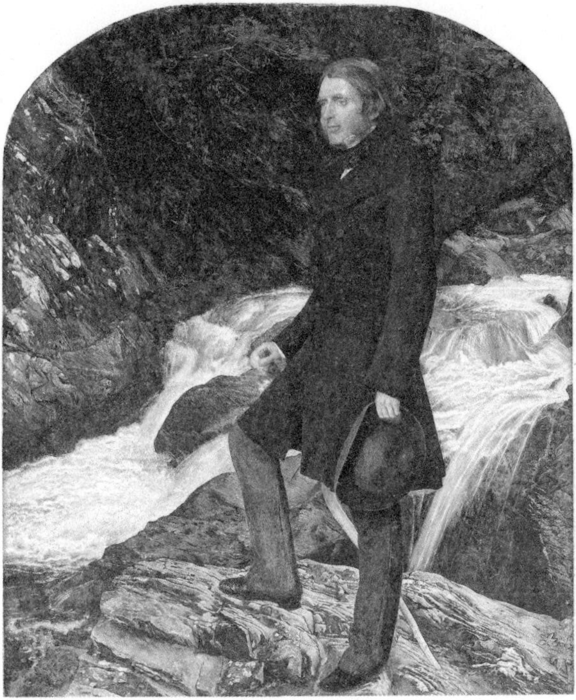

John Everett Millais, *John Ruskin*, 1853–1854
Oil on canvas, 28.1 × 23.9 inches | 71.3 × 60.8 cm

Editor's Note

When Ruskin wrote *Giotto and His Works in Padua* in the 1850s, the only available representations of Giotto's frescoes at the Scrovegni Chapel were black-and-white woodcuts. For the reader's reference, we have included one such woodcut (p. 14), but the original black-and-white reproductions have been replaced here with new color photographs of the frescoes. These photographs are gathered in a single plates section at the end of this volume and numbered I–XXXVIII to match Ruskin's descriptions of each panel.

The vast majority of the textual notes in this book are taken from the 1906 Cook and Wedderburn Library Edition of *The Works of John Ruskin*, which incorporates Ruskin's own notes and editorial notes from the 1900 Wedderburn-Allen edition. We have deleted notes that we regard as irrelevant to contemporary readers, and added some clarifications where we deemed them necessary. All of the editorial notes in this volume are followed by a year (1900, 1906, or 2018) to indicate whether they belong to the Wedderburn-Allen edition, Cook and Wedderburn's Library Edition, or are new to this edition. We have also converted the original footnotes into endnotes for greater readability.

We have striven to respect Ruskin's original text as far as possible; however, we have excised a short passage discussing the Arundel Society's woodcuts, as the prints have been replaced with photographs. We have maintained Ruskin's British spelling and nineteenth-century syntax, but in certain rare cases, we have made slight modifications to grammar and punctuation to reflect contemporary usage.

"The fiery cross of truth": John Ruskin's *Giotto and His Works in Padua*

Robert Hewison

Today, if you want to see Giotto's magnificent cycle of frescoes in the Arena Chapel in Padua, you have to book your timed ticket at least twenty-four hours in advance. You need to assemble in a group, and then wait for fifteen minutes in an air lock, to reduce humidity and dust. At last, you enter the image-crowded space. You have just twenty minutes, and then you are bundled out again, back into the twenty-first century.

It was not like that two hundred years ago, when discerning travelers began to rediscover Giotto's masterpiece. The chapel was privately owned, set in a grassy enclosure, and surrounded by vegetable gardens. It was all that survived of a palace built at the end of thirteenth century and demolished in 1827. Officially called the Scrovegni Chapel, after the family that built it, it took its more familiar name from the Roman arena that had once stood on the site. Murray's *Handbook for Travellers in Northern Italy* advised: "The key of the chapel is kept at the dwelling-house in the Arena, where the proprietor resides. Inquiry should also be made for the key of the sacristy, which is often kept locked."[1]

Having obtained the key and—to use John Ruskin's private phrase for money changing hands—"spoken Italian" with the custodian, the traveler would be free to enter a mildewed jewel box, dominated by the deep blue of Giotto's skies. Built in 1303, 20 meters long, only 8.5 meters wide, and 12.6 meters high, the chapel was consecrated in 1305, by which time it is assumed Giotto's decorations were in place.

Summoned from Florence, Giotto, not yet forty, was at the height of his powers. He supplied two narratives on the upper three tiers of his scheme, framed like a *bande dessiné*, beginning with the life of the Virgin Mary, and ending with the death and resurrection of her son, Jesus Christ. Christ sits in Judgment at the west end, while below the frescoes on the south and north walls a series of allegorical figures of the vices and virtues, painted in chiaroscuro, conduct a silent dialogue from above the pews.

Mid-nineteenth-century travelers might not have had to pass through air locks, but unless they were artists, they would have had no means of recording what they saw. Now, as the rich images in this book demonstrate, color photography makes the Arena Chapel accessible to all the world.

Then, it would have been seen by a few.

It was to remedy this that the Arundel Society was founded in London in 1849. It was a private organization, formed by a group of scholars and connoisseurs, among them the art critic John Ruskin. Their motives were didactic: to improve public taste and knowledge by going back to an earlier period of art history in order to demonstrate the future perfectibility of art. It was also conservationist (and covertly anti-Italian) in that much of the instructive art that it celebrated, including the Arena Chapel, was suffering serious neglect. The society's prospectus stated: "The materials of such instruction are abundant, but scattered, little accessible, and, in some instances, passing away. Of the frescoes of Giotto, Orcagna, Ghirlandajo, much of which has never been delineated, nor even properly described, is rapidly perishing."[2] At one point there were suggestions that the whole of the Arena Chapel might be brought to England.

For an annual subscription of a guinea (twenty-one shillings), members would receive a number of engraved reproductions selected by the society's committee. In the first three years seven plates, plus an illustrated translation of Vasari's life of Fra Angelico, were released, to about four hundred subscribers. The Arena Chapel project, however, was a new departure. Having issued an engraving of the Pietà scene in the chapel in 1851 (here, plate XXXV), it was decided to present the chapel as a whole. Partly because of the reproductive technology available, and partly because of the cost, the images would be rendered in black-and-white woodcuts, on paper tinted a parchment tone (see following page). A young artist studying at the Royal Academy Schools, William Oliver Williams, was commissioned to make reduced drawings in pen and ink in the chapel, and then transfer them to woodblocks, clamped together to give sufficient surface area. He also made full-scale tracings, so that his accuracy could be judged. The blocks were cut and printed by the well-established firm of Dalziel Brothers. The work went on until 1860, by which time the society had issued thirty-eight plates to subscribers. (Individual plates were also available at two shillings and sixpence to

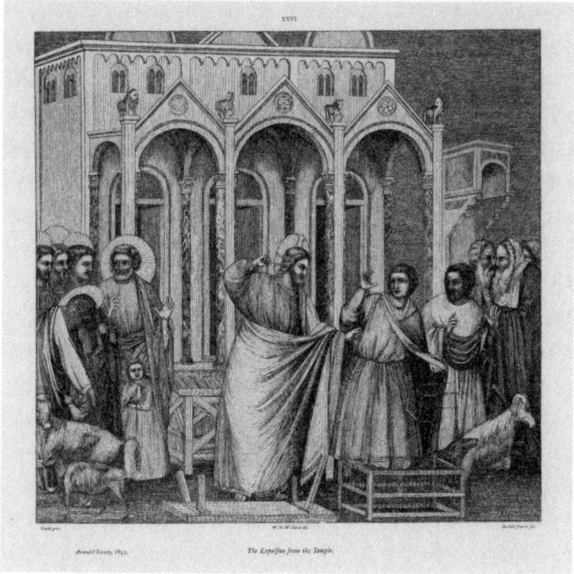

One of the original Arundel Society woodcuts depicting the Scrovegni Chapel frescoes.

members, and five shillings and sixpence to "strangers.") The series did not include the large Last Judgment on the west wall, or the allegorical figures on the bottom tier.

By commissioning their own artist, the society controlled the appearance of the woodcuts. A didactic emphasis on truth prevented the copyist "improving" the images, although some allowance was made for damaged areas. The length of time spent on the project, and the relative harshness of the woodcuts, help to explain why the project was not a commercial success. It was only when the society started issuing chromolithographs in 1856—a much more expensive process using multiple lithographic stones to create, as far as possible, accurate colors—that it became successful. By 1861 the Arundel Society had 1,200 members.

The choice of the Arena Chapel as its first major project was potentially controversial. Although taste was changing in their favor, the Italian painters of the early fourteenth century were regarded as "primitives." Ruskin used the term "the primitive schools of Sacred art" in his 1847 review of Lord Lindsay's pioneering *Sketches of the History of Christian Art*, which became a primary source for his commentary on the frescoes.[3] Fra Angelico was appreciated mainly for his religious sentiment, but while Giotto had been studied since the 1820s, and was recognized, along with Cimabue, as the "father" of Christian art, he was regarded as a naive predecessor of the great Raphael and the Renaissance masters.

This is one of the reasons why Ruskin was asked to write an introduction and a commentary on each plate. The project appears to have already been underway when he was commissioned in 1853. At thirty-four, Ruskin was a rising star. He had made his name with the first two volumes of *Modern Painters* in 1843 and 1846, and had just published the final volume of his three-volume cultural history *The Stones of Venice.* His introduction contains, in miniature, many of his arguments in these books. Because the woodcuts were being issued in parts, his commentary followed suit. Part one, the introduction and commentary on plates I–XIV, was written at the beginning of 1854, and published that year. Part two, the commentary on plates XV–XXII, was underway in April 1854, and published by the end of the same year. Part three, the commentary on the remaining plates, and with a punchy contemporary conclusion, did not appear until 1860.

In 1853 Ruskin had not seen the work attributed to Giotto in Assisi, or in Naples, as he frankly admitted. Indeed, he had had only brief experience of the Arena Chapel. Padua was the last town before Venice, so he regularly passed through, but his actual study of the frescoes was limited. In 1841 his diary notes that he had "felt much" in Padua, and seen frescoes by Giotto, but they were not necessarily those in the Arena Chapel. On his return from Venice in October 1845 he intended to visit the chapel, but was prevented by a fever. His diary on his 1846 journey is silent on the Arena Chapel, but in a revision to the 1848 edition of *Modern Painters*, volume two, he inserts a reference to the "rainbow play of brilliant harmonies" on the walls of the Arena Chapel,[4] and refers to the chapel in his 1847 review of Lord Lindsay. The one time we can properly place him in the Arena Chapel is on March 7 or 8, 1850. He indexed his diary, and "Arena" leads us to folio 55 of a smaller subsidiary notebook, "N." The notebook survives, but, frustratingly, most of folio 55 has been cut out.[5]

Ruskin does not disguise the fact that his commentary is based on memory and the woodcuts in front of him. To some extent, his prose makes up for the plainness of the images. He casts himself as an interpreter, but also a critic, prepared both to criticize the quality of the reproduction, for instance plate XXI, and, on occasion, Giotto himself (plate XXXVIII)—though he thought it right for the copyists not to "correct" the artist. Some of his errors derive from errors in the woodcuts, for instance his reference to the scourge in the hand of Jesus that was left out in plate XXVI (see p. 14).

Ruskin also admits his reliance on Lord Lindsay and the Italian architectural historian Pietro Selvatico. But his growing interest in illuminated manuscripts allowed him to overcome his Protestant suspicion of "Popery" and contribute information from a manuscript he was studying in the British Museum, *La vita de Joachy, e Anna, e Maria, e Yesu Christo*, a fourteenth-century Italian history of the Holy Family. He also contributed an illustration to support plate XXII from an illuminated antiphony in his own collection (p. 106). Scholarship has obviously progressed; many of the endnotes in this edition are taken from the 1906 edition prepared by E. T. Cook and Alexander Wedderburn for volume 24 of *The Works of John Ruskin*, the superb thirty-nine-volume "Library Edition" that makes modern Ruskin scholarship possible. Ruskin's reputation suffered a disastrous fall in the early twentieth century, and he remained a neglected, even disdained, figure until the 1960s, when American and British scholars began to recognize his profound influence on later social thought. At the same time, his interdisciplinarity, and his extraordinary gift for linking word and image, challenged academic orthodoxies. He is as critically appreciated now as much as he was universally admired at the time of his death in 1900.

Here, Ruskin is not afraid to pose the question that readers of this introduction might also ask: What is the use of Giotto to the nineteenth century, or, indeed, the twenty-first? Why republish in 1854, or 2018? His answer is that it is always necessary to strip away the encrustations of received ideas and conventional perceptions, in order to recover the sincerity of what he called "the innocent eye."[6] Ruskin is not being an antiquarian, but making a link between past and present in which Giotto, "a daring naturalist, in defiance of tradition, idealism, and formalism" (p. 40), becomes his ideal artist. Drawing on the character given to Giotto by Vasari in his sixteenth-century *Lives of the Artists*, Giotto is "healthy, kind, and active" (p. 34), full of practical sense and good humor, and above all a *craftsman*. Here Ruskin is thinking of his chapter "The Nature of Gothic" in the second volume of *The Stones of Venice*, where he attacks the enslavement of artists and craftsmen by classicism and industrialization. Giotto's love of color—so absent in the woodcuts, and so vital to Ruskin's taste—completes the naturalistic revolution that frees Western art of Byzantine formalism, and, combined with his use of mass, anticipates Titian.

Giotto fits neatly into Ruskin's view of Western art, developed in *Modern Painters* and elaborated in *The Stones of Venice*. As Byzantine art, with its Roman roots, falls into the formalism that will ruin the Renaissance, the northern spirit of the Gothic springs into life. Giotto's technical limitations are not important, since perfection, as Ruskin argued in "The Nature of Gothic," was a false value. In Ruskin's aesthetic, the early painters saw with a clarity of perception that had not been occluded by convention. This simplicity has the power to stimulate the imagination through symbolism as effectively as the realism of the art that was to follow.

Giotto offers inspiration, and continuity, right into the present. Just as Giotto was helped by the classical sculptures being discovered in his day, Giotto is a help to the Pre-Raphaelite Brotherhood, formed in 1848, which Ruskin was championing. The description of Giotto as "a daring naturalist, in defiance of tradition, idealism, and formalism" is applied directly to John Everett Millais, who had just painted Ruskin's portrait (and, as it happens, fallen in love with his wife). So Giotto is also, in a sense, a modern painter: "and thus the fiery cross of truth has been delivered from spirit to spirit, over the dust of intervening generations" (p. 40).

Ideas shift, and knowledge grows, but there is more than an antiquarian curiosity in revisiting this little-known work of Ruskin's. By the time it was finished, in 1860, he had come to see Giotto and his works in Padua in a context much wider than art history. His closing words, written in the same year that he published his attack on utilitarian political economy in *Unto This Last*, are pessimistic about the future for contemporary art. So long as modern society "can bear to see misery and squalor in its streets, it can neither invent nor accept human beauty in its pictures" (p. 134).

Is this 1860, or 2018? Such is "the fiery cross of truth."

1 *Handbook for Travellers in Northern Italy*, 4th ed. (London: John Murray, 1852), p. 293.
2 Quoted in Tim Hilton, *John Ruskin* (New Haven, Conn.: Yale University Press, 2002), p. 130.
3 John Ruskin, "The History of Christian Art" (1847), in *The Works of John Ruskin*, ed. E.T. Cook and Alexander Wedderburn, vol. 12 (London: George Allen, 1904), p. 174.
4 John Ruskin, *Modern Painters*, 2nd ed., vol. 2 (London: Smith, Elder, and Co., 1848), p. 209.
5 Facsimiles of Ruskin's Venetian diaries and notebooks can be seen online, courtesy the Ruskin Library, Lancaster University: http://www.lancaster.ac.uk/depts/ruskinlib/eSoV/index.html.
6 See, for example, John Ruskin, *The Elements of Drawing* (New York: Wiley & Halsted, 1858), pp. 22–23, n1.

Robert Hewison would like to thank Tanya Harrod for access to her DPhil thesis (as Tanya Ledger), "A Study of the Arundel Society," University of Oxford, 1978.

ADVERTISEMENT

To the First Edition (1854)

The following notice of Giotto has not been drawn up with any idea of attempting a history of his life. That history could only be written after a careful search through the libraries of Italy for all documents relating to the years during which he worked. I have no time for such search, or even for the examination of well-known and published materials; and have therefore merely collected, from the sources nearest at hand, such information as appeared absolutely necessary to render the series of Plates now published by the Arundel Society intelligible and interesting to those among its Members who have not devoted much time to the examination of medieval works. I have prefixed a few remarks on the relation of the art of Giotto to former and subsequent efforts, which I hope may be useful in preventing the general reader from either looking for what the painter never intended to give, or missing the points to which his endeavours were really directed.

J. R.

Giotto and His Works in Padua

1. Towards the close of the thirteenth century, Enrico Scrovegno, a noble Paduan, purchased, in his native city, the remains of the Roman Amphitheatre or Arena from the family of the Dalesmanini, to whom those remains had been granted by the Emperor Henry III of Germany in 1090. For the power of making this purchase, Scrovegno was in all probability indebted to his father, Reginald, who, for his avarice, is placed by Dante in the seventh circle of the *Inferno*, and regarded apparently as the chief of the usurers there, since he is the only one who addresses Dante.[1] The son, having possessed himself of the Roman ruin, or of the site which it had occupied, built himself a fortified palace upon the ground, and a chapel dedicated to the Annunciate Virgin.

2. This chapel, built in or about the year 1303,[2] appears to have been intended to replace one which had long existed on the spot; and in which, from the year 1278, an annual festival had been held on Lady Day, in which the Annunciation was represented in the manner of our English mysteries (and under the same title: "una sacra rappresentazione di quel *mistero*"), with dialogue, and music both vocal and instrumental. Scrovegno's purchase of the ground could not be allowed to interfere with the national custom; but he is reported by some writers to have rebuilt the chapel with greater costliness, in order, as far as possible, to efface the memory of his father's unhappy life. But Federici, in his history of the Cavalieri Godenti, supposes that Scrovegno was a member of that body, and was assisted by them in decorating

the new edifice. The order of Cavalieri Godenti was instituted in the beginning of the thirteenth century, to defend the "existence," as Selvatico states it, but more accurately the dignity, of the Virgin, against the various heretics by whom it was beginning to be assailed. Her knights were first called Cavaliers of St. Mary; but soon increased in power and riches to such a degree, that from their general habits of life, they received the nickname of the "Merry Brothers." Federici gives forcible reasons for his opinion that the Arena Chapel was employed in the ceremonies of their order; and Lord Lindsay observes that the fullness with which the history of the Virgin is recounted on its walls adds to the plausibility of his supposition.

3. Enrico Scrovegno was, however, towards the close of his life, driven into exile, and died at Venice in 1320. But he was buried in the chapel he had built; and has one small monument in the sacristy, as the founder of the building, in which he is represented under a Gothic niche, standing, with his hands clasped and his eyes raised; while behind the altar is his tomb, on which, as usual at the period, is a recumbent statue of him. The chapel itself may not unwarrantably be considered as one of the first efforts of Popery in resistance of the Reformation: for the Reformation, though not victorious till the sixteenth, began in reality in the thirteenth century; and the remonstrances of such bishops as our own Grosseteste,[3] the martyrdoms of the Albigenses in the Dominican crusades, and the murmurs of those "heretics" against

whose aspersions of the majesty of the Virgin this chivalrous order of the Cavalieri Godenti was instituted, were as truly the signs of the approach of a new era in religion, as the opponent work of Giotto on the walls of the Arena was a sign of the approach of a new era in art.

4. The chapel having been founded, as stated above, in 1303, Giotto appears to have been summoned to decorate its interior walls about the year 1306—summoned, as being at that time the acknowledged master of painting in Italy. By what steps he had risen to this unquestioned eminence it is difficult to trace; for the records of his life, strictly examined, and freed from the verbiage and conjecture of artistical history, nearly reduce themselves to a list of the cities of Italy where he painted, and to a few anecdotes, of little meaning in themselves, and doubly pointless in the fact of most of them being inheritances of the whole race of painters, and related successively of all in whose biographies the public have deigned to take an interest. There is even question as to the date of his birth;[4] Vasari stating him to have been born in 1276, while Baldinucci, on the internal evidence derived from Vasari's own narrative, throws the date back ten years.[5] I believe, however, that Vasari is most probably accurate in his first main statement; and that his errors, always numerous, are in the subsequent and minor particulars. It is at least undoubted truth that Giotto was born, and passed the years of childhood, at Vespignano, about fourteen miles north of Florence, on the road to Bologna. Few travellers can forget the peculiar landscape of that

district of the Apennine. As they ascend the hill which rises from Florence to the lowest break in the ridge at Fiesole, they pass continually beneath the walls of villas bright in perfect luxury, and beside cypress hedges, enclosing fair terraced gardens, where the masses of oleander and magnolia, motionless as leaves in a picture, inlay alternately upon the blue sky their branching lightness of pale rose colour, and deep green breadth of shade, studded with balls of budding silver, and showing at intervals through their framework of rich leaf and rubied flower, the far-away bends of the Arno beneath its slopes of olive, and the purple peaks of the Carrara mountains, tossing themselves against the western distance, where the streaks of motionless clouds burn above the Pisan sea. The traveller passes the Fiesolan ridge, and all is changed. The country is on a sudden lonely. Here and there indeed are seen the scattered houses of a farm grouped gracefully upon the hillsides—here and there a fragment of tower upon a distant rock; but neither gardens, nor flowers, nor glittering palace walls, only a grey extent of mountain ground, tufted irregularly with ilex and olive: a scene not sublime, for its forms are subdued and low; not desolate, for its valleys are full of sown fields and tended pastures; not rich nor lovely, but sunburnt and sorrowful; becoming wilder every instant as the road winds into its recesses, ascending still, until the higher woods, now partly oak and partly pine, drooping back from the central crest of the Apennine, leave a pastoral wilderness of scathed rock and arid grass, withered away here by frost, and there by strange lambent tongues of earth-fed fire.[6] Giotto passed the first ten years of his life, a shepherd boy, among these hills; was found by Cimabue, near his native village, drawing one of his sheep upon a smooth stone; was yielded up by his father, "a simple person, a labourer of the earth," to the guardianship of the painter, who, by his own work, had already made the streets of Florence ring with joy; attended him to Florence, and became his disciple.

We may fancy the glance of the boy, when he and Cimabue stood side by side on the ridge of Fiesole, and for the first time he saw the flowering thickets of the Val d'Arno; and deep beneath, the innumerable towers of the City of the Lily, the depths of his own heart yet hiding the fairest of them all. Another ten years passed over him, and he was chosen from among the painters of Italy to decorate the Vatican.

5. The account given us by Vasari of the mode of his competition on this occasion, is one of the few anecdotes of him which seem to be authentic (especially as having given rise to an Italian proverb), and it has also great point and value. I translate Vasari's words literally:

> This work (his paintings in the Campo Santo of Pisa) acquired for him, both in the city and externally, so much fame, that the Pope Benedict IX sent a certain one of his courtiers into Tuscany, to see what sort of a man Giotto was, and what was the quality of his works, he (the pope) intending to have some

paintings executed in St. Peter's; which courtier, coming to see Giotto, and hearing that there were other masters in Florence who excelled in painting and in mosaic, spoke, in Siena, to many masters; then, having received drawings from them, he came to Florence; and having gone one morning into Giotto's shop as he was at work, explained the pope's mind to him, and in what way he wished to avail himself of his powers, and finally requested from him a little piece of drawing to send to his Holiness. Giotto, who was most courteous, took a leaf (of vellum?), and upon this, with a brush dipped in red, fixing his arm to his side, to make it as the limb of a pair of compasses, and turning his hand, made a circle so perfect in measure and outline that it was a wonder to see: which having done, he said to the courtier, with a smile, "There is the drawing." He, thinking himself mocked, said, "Shall I have no other drawing than this?" "This is enough, and too much," answered Giotto; "send it with the others: you will see if it will be understood." The ambassador, seeing that he could not get anything else, took his leave with small satisfaction, doubting whether he had not been made a jest of. However, when he sent to the pope the other drawings, and the names of those who had made them, he sent also that of Giotto, relating the way in which he had held himself in drawing his circle, without moving his arm, and without compasses. Whence the pope, and many intelligent courtiers, knew how much

Giotto overpassed in excellence all the other painters of his time. Afterwards, the thing becoming known, the proverb arose from it: "Thou art rounder than the O of Giotto"; which it is still in custom to say to men of the grosser clay; for the proverb is pretty, not only on account of the accident of its origin, but because it has a double meaning, "round" being taken in Tuscany to express not only circular form, but slowness and grossness of wit.

6. Such is the account of Vasari, which, at the first reading, might be gravely called into question, seeing that the paintings at Pisa, to which he ascribes the sudden extent of Giotto's reputation, have been proved to be the work of Francesco da Volterra;[7] and since, moreover, Vasari has even mistaken the name of the pope, and written Benedict IX for Boniface VIII. But the story itself must, I think, be true; and, rightly understood, it is singularly interesting. I say, rightly understood; for Lord Lindsay supposes the circle to have been mechanically drawn by turning the sheet of vellum under the hand, as now constantly done for the sake of speed at schools. But neither do Vasari's words bear this construction, nor would the drawing so made have borne the slightest testimony to Giotto's power. Vasari says distinctly, "and turning his hand" (or, as I should rather read it, "with a sweep of his hand"[8]), not "turning the vellum"; neither would a circle produced in so mechanical a manner have borne distinct witness to anything

except the draughtsman's mechanical ingenuity; and Giotto had too much common sense, and too much courtesy, to send the pope a drawing which did not really contain the evidence he required. Lord Lindsay has been misled also by his own careless translation of "pennello tinto di roffo" ("a *brush* dipped in red") by the word "crayon." It is easy to draw the mechanical circle with a crayon, but by no means easy with a brush. I have not the slightest doubt that Giotto drew the circle as a painter naturally would draw it; that is to say that he set the vellum upright on the wall or panel before him, and then, steadying his arm firmly against his side, drew the circular line with one sweeping but firm revolution of his hand, holding the brush long. Such a feat as this is completely possible to a well-disciplined painter's hand, but utterly impossible to any other; and the circle so drawn was the most convincing proof Giotto could give of his decision of eye and perfectness of practice.

7. Still, even when thus understood, there is much in the anecdote very curious. Here is a painter requested by the head of the Church to execute certain religious paintings, and the only qualification for the task of which he deigns to demonstrate his possession is executive skill. Nothing is said, and nothing appears to be thought, of expression, or invention, or devotional sentiment. Nothing is required but firmness of hand. And here arises the important question: Did Giotto know that this was all that was looked for by his religious patrons? And is there occult satire in the example of his art which

he sends them? Or does the founder of sacred painting mean to tell us that he holds his own power to consist merely in firmness of hand, secured by long practice? I cannot satisfy myself on this point: but yet it seems to me that we may safely gather two conclusions from the words of the master, "It is enough, and more than enough." The first, that Giotto had indeed a profound feeling of the value of *precision* in all art; and that we may use the full force of his authority to press the truth, of which it is so difficult to persuade the hasty workmen of modern times, that the difference between right and wrong lies within the breadth of a line; and that the most perfect power and genius are shown by the accuracy which disdains error, and the faithfulness which fears it.

8. And the second conclusion is that whatever Giotto's imaginative powers might be, he was proud to be a good *workman*, and willing to be considered by others only as such. There might lurk, as has been suggested, some satire in the message to the pope, and some consciousness in his own mind of faculties higher than those of draughtsmanship. I cannot tell how far these hidden feelings existed; but the more I see of living artists, and learn of departed ones, the more I am convinced that the highest strength of genius is generally marked by strange unconsciousness of its own modes of operation, and often by no small scorn of the best results of its exertion. The inferior mind intently watches its own processes, and dearly values its own produce; the master mind is intent on other things than itself, and cares little for the

fruits of a toil which it is apt to undertake rather as a law of life than a means of immortality. It will sing at a feast, or retouch an old play, or paint a dark wall, for its daily bread, anxious only to be honest in its fulfilment of its pledges or its duty, and careless that future ages will rank it among the gods.

9. I think it unnecessary to repeat here any other of the anecdotes commonly related of Giotto, as, separately taken, they are quite valueless. Yet much may be gathered from their general *tone*. It is remarkable that they are, almost without exception, records of good-humoured jests, involving or illustrating some point of practical good sense:[9] and by comparing this general colour of the reputation of Giotto with the actual character of his designs, there cannot remain the smallest doubt that his mind was one of the most healthy, kind, and active that ever informed a human frame. His love of beauty was entirely free from weakness; his love of truth untinged by severity; his industry constant, without impatience; his workmanship accurate, without formalism; his temper serene, and yet playful; his imagination exhaustless, without extravagance; and his faith firm, without superstition. I do not know, in the annals of art, such another example of happy, practical, unerring, and benevolent power.

I am certain that this is the estimate of his character which must be arrived at by an attentive study of his works, and of the few data which remain respecting his life; but I shall not here endeavour to give proof of its truth, because I believe the subject has been exhaustively treated by Rumohr and Förster, whose essays on the works and character of Giotto will doubtless be translated into English, as the interest of the English public in medieval art increases. I shall therefore here only endeavour briefly to sketch the relation which Giotto held to the artists who preceded and followed him, a relation still imperfectly understood; and then, as briefly, to indicate the general course of his labours in Italy, as far as may be necessary for understanding the value of the series in the Arena Chapel.

10. The art of Europe, between the fifth and thirteenth centuries, divides itself essentially into two great branches, one springing from, the other grafted on, the old Roman stock. The first is the Roman art itself, prolonged in a languid and degraded condition, and becoming at last a mere formal system, centered at the seat of the Eastern Empire, and thence generally called Byzantine. The other is the barbarous and incipient art of the Gothic nations, more or less coloured by Roman or Byzantine influence, and gradually increasing in life and power.

Generally speaking, the Byzantine art, although manifesting itself only in perpetual repetitions, becoming every day more cold and formal, yet preserved reminiscences of design originally noble, and traditions of execution originally perfect.

Generally speaking, the Gothic art, although becoming every day more powerful, presented the most ludicrous experiments of infantile imagination, and the most rude efforts of untaught manipulation.

Hence, if any superior mind arose in Byzantine art, it had before it models which suggested or recorded a perfection they did not themselves possess; and the superiority of the individual mind would probably be shown in a more sincere and living treatment of the subjects ordained for repetition by the canons of the schools.

In the art of the Goth, the choice of subject was unlimited, and the style of design so remote from all perfection, as not always even to point out clearly the direction in which advance could be made. The strongest minds which appear in that art are therefore generally manifested by redundance of imagination, and sudden refinement of touch, whether of pencil or chisel, together with unexpected starts of effort or flashes of knowledge in accidental directions, gradually forming various national styles.

11. Of these comparatively independent branches of art, the greatest is, as far as I know, the French sculpture of the thirteenth century. No words can give any idea of the magnificent redundance of its imaginative power, or of the perpetual beauty of even its smallest incidental designs. But this very richness of sculptural invention prevented the French from cultivating their powers of painting, except in illumination (of which art they were the acknowledged masters), and in glass painting. Their exquisite gift of fretting their stonework with inexhaustible wealth of sculpture prevented their feeling the need of figure design on coloured surfaces.

The style of architecture prevalent in Italy at the same period presented, on the contrary, large blank surfaces, which could only be rendered interesting by covering them with mosaic or painting.

The Italians were not at the time capable of doing this for themselves, and mosaicists were brought from Constantinople, who covered the churches of Italy with a sublime monotony of Byzantine traditions. But the Gothic blood was burning in the Italian veins; and the Florentines and Pisans could not rest content in the formalism of the Eastern splendour. The first innovator was, I believe, Giunta of Pisa, the second Cimabue, the third Giotto; the last only being a man of power enough to effect a complete revolution in the artistic principles of his time.

12. He, however, began, like his master Cimabue, with a perfect respect for his Byzantine models; and his paintings for a long time consisted only of repetitions of the Byzantine subjects, softened in treatment, enriched in number of figures, and enlivened in gesture. Afterwards he invented subjects of his own. The manner and degree of the changes which he at first effected could only be properly understood by actual comparison of his designs with the Byzantine originals;[10] but in default of the means of such a comparison, it may be generally stated that the innovations of Giotto consisted in the introduction, A, of gayer or lighter colours; B, of broader masses; and, C, of more careful imitation of nature than existed in the works of his predecessors.

(A) *Greater lightness of colour*. This was partly in compliance with a tendency which was beginning to manifest itself even before Giotto's time. Over the whole of

Northern Europe, the colouring of the eleventh and early twelfth centuries had been pale: in manuscripts, principally composed of pale red, green, and yellow, blue being sparingly introduced (earlier still, in the eighth and ninth centuries, the letters had often been coloured with black and yellow only). Then, in the close of the twelfth and throughout the thirteenth century, the great system of perfect colour was in use; solemn and deep; composed strictly, in all its leading masses, of the colours revealed by God from Sinai as the noblest;[11]—blue, purple, and scarlet, with gold (other hues, chiefly green, with white and black, being used in points of small masses, to relieve the main colours). In the early part of the fourteenth century the colours begin to grow paler; about 1330 the style is already completely modified; and at the close of the fourteenth century the colour is quite pale and delicate.

I have not carefully examined the colouring of early Byzantine work; but it seems always to have been comparatively dark, and in manuscripts is remarkably so; Giotto's paler colouring, therefore, though only part of the great European system, was rendered notable by its stronger contrast with the Byzantine examples.

(B) *Greater breadth of mass.* It had been the habit of the Byzantines to break up their draperies by a large number of minute folds. Norman and Romanesque sculpture showed much of the same character. Giotto melted all these folds into broad masses of colour; so that his compositions have sometimes almost a Titianesque look in this particular. This innovation was a healthy one, and led to very noble results when followed up by succeeding artists: but in many of Giotto's compositions the figures become ludicrously cumbrous, from the exceeding simplicity of the terminal lines, and massiveness of unbroken form. The manner was copied in illuminated manuscripts with great disadvantage, as it was unfavourable to minute ornamentation. The French never adopted it in either branch of art, nor did any other Northern school; minute and sharp folds of the robes remaining characteristic of Northern (more especially of Flemish and German) design down to the latest times, giving a great superiority to the French and Flemish illuminated work, and causing a proportionate inferiority in their large pictorial efforts. Even Rubens and Van Dyck cannot free themselves from a certain meanness and minuteness in disposition of drapery.

(C) *Close imitation of nature*. In this one principle lay Giotto's great strength, and the entire secret of the revolution he effected. It was not by greater learning, nor by the discovery of new theories of art, not by greater taste, nor by "ideal" principles of selection, that he became the head of the progressive schools of Italy. It was simply by being interested in what was going on around him, by substituting the gestures of living men for conventional attitudes, and portraits of living men for conventional faces, and incidents of everyday life for conventional circumstances, that he became great, and the master of the great. Giotto was to his contemporaries precisely what Millais is to *his* contemporaries—a daring naturalist, in defiance of tradition, idealism, and formalism. The Giottesque movement in the fourteenth, and Pre-Raphaelite movement in the nineteenth centuries, are precisely similar in bearing and meaning: both being the protests of vitality against mortality, of spirit against letter, and of truth against tradition: and both, which is the more singular, literally links in one unbroken chain of feeling; for exactly as Nicola Pisano and Giotto were helped by the classical sculptures discovered in their time, the Pre-Raphaelites have been helped by the works of Nicola and Giotto at Pisa and Florence: and thus the fiery cross of truth has been delivered from spirit to spirit, over the dust of intervening generations.

13. But what, it may be said by the reader, is the use of the works of Giotto to *us*? They may indeed have been wonderful for their time, and of infinite use in that time; but since, after Giotto, came Leonardo and Correggio, what is the use of going back to the ruder art, and republishing it in the year 1854? Why should we fret ourselves to dig down to the root of the tree, when we may at once enjoy its fruit and foliage? I answer, first, that in all matters relating to human intellect, it is a great thing to have hold of the root: that at least we ought to see it, and taste it, and handle it; for it often happens that the root is wholesome when the leaves, however fair, are useless or poisonous. In nine cases out of ten, the first expression of an idea is the most valuable: the idea may afterwards be polished and softened, and made more attractive to

the general eye; but the first expression of it has a freshness and brightness, like the flash of a native crystal compared to the lustre of glass that has been melted and cut. And in the second place, we ought to measure the value of art less by its executive than by its moral power. Giotto was not indeed one of the most accomplished painters, but he was one of the greatest men who ever lived. He was the first master of his time, in architecture as well as in painting; he was the friend of Dante, and the undisputed interpreter of religious truth, by means of painting, over the whole of Italy. The works of such a man may not be the best to set before children in order to teach them drawing; but they assuredly should be studied with the greatest care by all who are interested in the history of the human mind.

14. One point more remains to be noticed respecting him. As far as I am aware, he never painted profane subjects. All his important existing works are exclusively devoted to the illustration of Christianity. This was not a result of his own peculiar feeling or determination; it was a necessity of the period. Giotto appears to have considered himself simply as a workman, at the command of any employer, for any kind of work, however humble. "In the sixty-third novel of Franco Sacchetti we read that a stranger, suddenly entering Giotto's study, threw down a shield, and departed, saying, 'Paint me my arms on that shield.' Giotto looking after him, exclaimed, 'Who is he? What is he? He says, "Paint me my arms," as if he was one of the Bardi. What arms does he bear?'"[12] But at the time

of Giotto's eminence, art was never employed on a great scale except in the service of religion; nor has it ever been otherwise employed, except in declining periods. I do not mean to draw any severe conclusion from this fact; but it is a fact nevertheless, which ought to be very distinctly stated, and very carefully considered. All *progressive* art hitherto has been religious art; and commencements of the periods of decline are accurately marked, in illumination, by its employment on romances instead of psalters; and in painting, by its employment on mythology or profane history instead of sacred history. Yet perhaps I should rather have said, on *heathen mythology* instead of *Christian mythology*; for this latter term—first used, I believe, by Lord Lindsay—is more applicable to the subjects of the early painters than that of "sacred *history*." Of all the virtues commonly found in the higher orders of human mind, that of a stern and just respect for truth seems to be the rarest; so that while self-denial, and courage, and charity, and religious zeal, are displayed in their utmost degrees by myriads of saints and heroes, it is only once in a century that a man appears whose word may be implicitly trusted, and who, in the relation of a plain fact, will not allow his prejudices or his pleasure to tempt him to some colouring or distortion of it. Hence the portions of sacred history which have been the constant subjects of fond popular contemplation have, in the lapse of ages, been encumbered with fictitious detail; and their various historians seem to have considered the exercise of their imagination innocent, and even meritorious, if they could increase either the vividness of conception or the sincerity of belief in their readers. A due consideration of that well-known weakness of the popular mind, which renders a statement credible in proportion to the multitude of local and circumstantial details which accompany it, may lead us to look with some indulgence on the errors, however fatal in their issue to the cause they were intended to advance, of those weak teachers, who thought the acceptance of their general statements of Christian doctrine cheaply won by the help of some simple (and generally absurd) inventions of detail respecting the life of the Virgin or the Apostles.

15. Indeed, I can hardly imagine the Bible to be ever read with true interest, unless, in our reading, we feel some longing for further knowledge of the minute incidents of the life of Christ—for some records of those things, which "if they had been written every one,"[13] the world could not have contained the books that should be written: and they who have once felt this thirst for further truth, may surely both conceive and pardon the earnest questioning of simple disciples (who knew not, as we do, how much had been indeed revealed), and measure with some justice the strength of the temptation which betrayed these teachers into adding to the word of Revelation. Together with this specious and subtle influence, we must allow for the instinct of imagination exerting itself in the acknowledged embellishment of beloved truths. If we reflect how much, even in this age

of accurate knowledge, the visions of Milton have become confused in the minds of many persons with scriptural facts, we shall rather be surprised that in an age of legends so little should be added to the Bible, than that occasionally we should be informed of important circumstances in sacred history with the collateral warning, "This Moses spake not of."[14]

More especially in the domain of painting, it is surprising to see how strictly the early workmen confined themselves to representations of the same series of scenes; how little of pictorial embellishment they usually added; and how, even in the positions and gestures of figures, they strove to give the idea rather of their having seen the *fact*, than imagined a picturesque treatment of it. Often, in examining early art, we mistake conscientiousness for servility, and attribute to the absence of invention what was indeed the result of the earnestness of faith.

Nor, in a merely artificial point of view, is it less important to note that the greatest advance in power was made when painters had few subjects to treat. The day has perhaps come when genius should be shown in the discovery of perpetually various interest amidst the incidents of actual life; and the absence of inventive capacity is very assuredly proved by the narrow selection of subjects which commonly appear on the walls of our exhibitions. But yet it is to be always remembered that more originality may be shown in giving interest to a well-known subject than in discovering a new one; that the greatest poets whom the world has seen have been contented to retouch and exalt the creations of their predecessors; and that the painters of the Middle Ages reached their utmost power by unweariedly treading a narrow circle of sacred subjects.

16. Nothing is indeed more notable in the history of art than the exact balance of its point of excellence, in all things, midway between servitude and licence. Thus, in choice and treatment of subject, it became paralysed among the Byzantines, by being mercilessly confined to a given series of scenes, and to a given mode of representing them. Giotto gave it partial liberty and incipient life; by the artists who succeeded him the range of its scenery was continually extended, and the severity of its style slowly softened to perfection. But the range was still, in some degree, limited by the necessity of its continual subordination to religious purposes; and the style, though softened, was still chaste, and though tender, self-restrained. At last came the period of licence: the artist chose his subjects from the lowest scenes of human life, and let loose his passions in their portraiture. And the kingdom of art passed away.

As if to direct us to the observation of this great law, there is a curious visible type of it in the progress of ornamentation in manuscripts, corresponding with the various changes in the higher branch of art. In the course of the twelfth and early thirteenth centuries, the ornamentation, though often full of high feeling and fantasy, is sternly enclosed within limiting border-lines—at first, severe squares, oblongs, or triangles. As the grace of the ornamentation advances, these border-lines are softened and broken into various curves, and the inner design begins here and there to overpass them. Gradually this emergence becomes more constant, and the lines which thus escape throw themselves into curvatures expressive of the most exquisite concurrence of freedom with self-restraint. At length the restraint vanishes, the freedom changes consequently into licence, and the page is covered with exuberant, irregular, and foolish extravagances of leafage and line.

17. It only remains to be noticed that the circumstances of the time at which Giotto appeared were peculiarly favourable to the development of genius; owing partly to the simplicity of the methods of practice, and partly to the naïveté with which art was commonly regarded. Giotto, like all the great painters of the period, was merely a travelling decorator of walls, at so much a day; having at Florence a *bottega*, or workshop, for the production and sale of small tempera pictures. There were no such things as "studios" in those days. An artist's "studies" were over by the time he was eighteen; after that he was a *lavoratore*, "labourer," a man who knew his business, and produced certain works of known value for a known price; being troubled with no philosophical abstractions, shutting himself up in no wise for the reception of inspirations; receiving, indeed, a good many, as a matter of course—just as he received the sunbeams which came in at his window, the light which he

worked by—in either case, without mouthing about it, or much concerning himself as to the nature of it. Not troubled by critics either; satisfied that his work was well done, and that people would find it out to be well done; but not vain of it, nor more profoundly vexed at its being found fault with, than a good saddler would be by some-one's saying his last saddle was uneasy in the seat. Not, on the whole, much molested by critics, but generally understood by the men of sense, his neighbours and friends, and permitted to have his own way with the walls he had to paint, as being, on the whole, an authority about walls; receiving at the same time a good deal of daily encouragement and comfort in the simple admiration of the populace, and in the general sense of having done good, and painted what no man could look upon without being the better for it.

18. Thus he went, a serene labourer, throughout the length and breadth of Italy. For the first ten years of his life, a shepherd; then a student, perhaps for five or six; then already in Florence, setting himself to his life's task; and called as a master to Rome when he was only twenty. There he painted the principal chapel of St. Peter's, and worked in mosaic also, no handicrafts that had colour or form for their objects seeming unknown to him. Then returning to Florence, he painted Dante, about the year 1300,[15] the thirty-fifth year of Dante's life, the twenty-fourth of his own; and designed the façade of the Duomo, on the death of its former architect, Arnolfo.[16] Some six years afterwards he went to Padua, there painting the

chapel which is the subject of our present study, and many other churches. Thence south again, to Assisi, where he painted half the walls and vaults of the great convent that stretches itself along the slopes of the Perugian hills, and various other minor works on his way there and back to Florence. Staying in his native city but a little while, he engaged himself in other tasks at Ferrara, Verona, and Ravenna, and at last at Avignon, where be became acquainted with Petrarch—working there for some three years, from 1324 to 1327;[17] and then passed rapidly through Florence and Orvieto on his way to Naples, where "he received the kindest welcome from the good king Robert.... The king, ever partial to men of mind and genius, took especial delight in Giotto's society, and used frequently to visit him while working in the Castello dell' Uovo, taking pleasure in watching his pencil and listening to his discourse; 'and Giotto,' says Vasari, 'who had ever his repartee and bonmot ready, held him there, fascinated at once with the magic of his pencil and pleasantry of his tongue.' We are not told the length of his sojourn at Naples, but it must have been for a considerable period, judging from the quantity of works he executed there. He had certainly returned to Florence in 1332."[18] There he was immediately appointed "chief master" of the works of the Duomo, then in progress, "with a yearly salary of one hundred gold florins, and the privilege of citizenship." He designed the Campanile, in a more perfect form than that which now exists; for his intended spire, 150 feet in height, never was erected. He, however, modelled the bas-reliefs for the base of the building, and sculptured two of them with his own hand. It was afterwards completed, with the exception of the spire, according to his design; but he only saw its foundations laid, and its first marble story rise. He died at Florence, on the 8th of January, 1337,[19] full of honour; happy, perhaps, in departing at the zenith of his strength, when his eye had not become dim, nor his natural force abated.[20] He was buried in the cathedral, at the angle nearest his campanile; and thus the tower, which is the chief grace of his native city, may be regarded as his own sepulchral monument.

19. I may refer the reader to the close of Lord Lindsay's letter on Giotto,[21] from which I have drawn most of the particulars above stated, for a very beautiful sketch of his character and his art. Of the real rank of that art, in the abstract, I do not feel myself capable of judging accurately, not having seen his finest works (at Assisi and Naples),[22] nor carefully studied even those at Florence. But I may be permitted to point out one or two peculiar characteristics in it which have always struck me forcibly.

In the first place, Giotto never finished highly. He was not, indeed, a loose or sketchy painter, but he was by no means a delicate one. His lines, as the story of the circle would lead us to expect, are always firm, but they are never fine. Even in his smallest tempera pictures the touch is bold and somewhat heavy: in his fresco work the handling is much broader than that of contemporary painters, corresponding somewhat to the character of many of the figures, representing plain, masculine kind of people, and never reaching anything like the ideal refinement of the conceptions even of Benozzo Gozzoli, far less of Angelico or Francia. For this reason, the character of his painting is better expressed by bold wood engravings than in general it is likely to be by any other means.

Again, he was a very noble colourist; and in his peculiar feeling for breadth of hue resembled Titian more than any other of the Florentine school. That is to say, had he been born two centuries later, when the art of painting was fully known, I believe he would have treated his subjects much more like Titian than like Raphael; in fact, the frescoes of Titian in the chapel beside the Church of St. Antonio at Padua, are, in all technical qualities, and in many of their conceptions, almost exactly what I believe Giotto would have done, had he lived in Titian's time. As it was, he of course never attained either richness or truth of colour; but in serene brilliancy he is not easily rivalled; invariably massing his hues in large fields, limiting them firmly, and then filling them with subtle gradation. He had the Venetian fondness for bars and stripes, not unfrequently casting barred colours obliquely across the draperies of an upright figure, from side to side (as very notably in the dress of one of the musicians who are playing to the dancing of Herodias's daughter, in one of his frescoes at Santa Croce); and this predilection was mingled with the truly medieval love of *quartering*.[23] The figure of the Madonna in the small tempera pictures in the Academy at Florence is always completely divided into two narrow segments by her dark-blue robe.

20. And this is always to be remembered in looking at any engravings from the works of Giotto; for the injury they sustain in being deprived of their colour is far greater than in the case of later designers. All works produced in the fourteenth century agree in being more or less decorative; they were intended in most instances to be subservient to architectural effect, and were executed in the manner best calculated to produce a striking impression when they were seen in a mass. The painted wall and the painted window were part and parcel of one magnificent whole; and it is as unjust to the work of Giotto, or of any contemporary artist, to take out a single feature from the series, and represent it in black and white on a separate page, as it would be to take out a compartment of a noble coloured window, and engrave it in the same manner. What is at once refined and effective, if seen at the intended distance in unison with the rest of the work, becomes coarse and insipid when seen isolated and near; and the more skilfully the design is arranged, so as to give full value to the colours which are introduced in it, the more blank and cold will it become when it is deprived of them.

In our modern art we have indeed lost sight of one great principle which regulated that of the Middle Ages, namely, that chiaroscuro and colour are incompatible in their highest degrees. Wherever chiaroscuro enters, colour must lose some of its brilliancy. There is no *shade* in a rainbow, nor in an opal, nor in a piece of mother-of-pearl, nor in a well-designed painted window; only various hues of perfect colour. The best pictures, by subduing their colour and conventionalizing their chiaroscuro, reconcile both in their diminished degrees; but a perfect light and shade cannot be given without considerable loss of liveliness in colour. Hence the supposed inferiority of Tintoretto to Titian. Tintoretto is, in reality, the greater colourist of the two; but he could not bear to falsify his light and shadow enough to set off his colour. Titian nearly strikes the exact mean between the painted glass of the thirteenth century and Rembrandt; while Giotto closely approaches the system of painted glass, and hence his compositions lose grievously by being translated into black and white.

21. But even his chiaroscuro, however subdued, is not without a peculiar charm; and the accompanying engravings possess a marked superiority over all that have hitherto been made from the works of this painter, in rendering this chiaroscuro, as far as possible, together with the effect of the local colours. The true appreciation of art has been retarded for many years by the habit of trusting to outlines as a sufficient expression of the sentiment of compositions; whereas in all truly great designs, of whatever age, it is never the outline, but the disposition of the masses, whether of shade or colour, on which the real power of the work depends. For instance, in plate III (The Angel Appears to Anna), the interest of

the composition depends entirely upon the broad shadows which fill the spaces of the chamber, and of the external passage in which the attendant is sitting. This shade explains the whole scene in a moment; gives prominence to the curtain and coverlid of the homely bed, and the rude chest and trestles which form the poor furniture of the house; and conducts the eye easily and instantly to the three figures, which, had the scene been expressed in outline only, we should have had to trace out with some care and difficulty among the pillars of the loggia and folds of the curtains. So also the relief of the faces in light against the dark sky is of peculiar value in the compositions X and XII.

22. The *drawing* of Giotto is, of course, exceedingly faulty. His knowledge of the human figure is deficient; and this, the necessary drawback in all works of the period, occasions an extreme difficulty in rendering them faithfully in an engraving. For wherever there is good and legitimate drawing, the ordinary education of a modern draughtsman enables him to copy it with tolerable accuracy; but when once the true forms of nature are departed from, it is by no means easy to express *exactly* the error, and *no more than* the error, of his original. In most cases modern copyists try to modify or hide the weaknesses of the old art—by which procedure they very often wholly lose its spirit, and only half redeem its defects; the results being, of course, at once false as representations, and intrinsically valueless. And just as it requires great courage and skill in an interpreter to speak

out honestly all the rough and rude words of the first speaker, and to translate deliberately and resolutely, in the face of attentive men, the expressions of his weakness or impatience; so it requires at once the utmost courage and skill in a copyist to trace faithfully the failures of an imperfect master, in the front of modern criticism, and against the inborn instincts of his own hand and eye. And let him do the best he can, he will still find that the grace and life of his original are continually flying off like a vapour, while all the faults he has so diligently copied sit rigidly staring him in the face—a terrible *caput mortuum*. It is very necessary that this should be well understood by the members of the Arundel Society, when they hear their engravings severely criticized. It is easy to produce an agreeable engraving by graceful infidelities; but the entire endeavour of the draughtsmen employed by this society has been to obtain accurately the character of the original: and he who never proposes to himself to rise *above* the work he is copying, must most assuredly often fall beneath it. Such fall is the inherent and inevitable penalty on all absolute copyism; and wherever the copy is made with sincerity, the fall must be endured with patience. It will never be an utter or a degrading fall; that is reserved for those who, like vulgar translators, wilfully quit the hand of their master, and have no strength of their own.

23. Lastly. It is especially to be noticed that these works of Giotto, in common with all others of the period, are independent of all the inferior sources of pictorial interest.

They never show the slightest attempt at imitative realization: they are simple suggestions of ideas, claiming no regard except for the inherent value of the thoughts. There is no filling of the landscape with variety of scenery, architecture, or incident, as in the works of Benozzo Gozzoli or Perugino; no wealth of jewellery and gold spent on the dresses of the figures, as in the delicate labours of Angelico or Gentile da Fabriano. The background is never more than a few gloomy masses of rock, with a tree or two, and perhaps a fountain; the architecture is merely what is necessary to explain the scene; the dresses are painted sternly on the "heroic" principle of Sir Joshua Reynolds—that drapery is to be "drapery, and nothing more"—there is no silk, nor velvet, nor distinguishable material of any kind: the whole power of the picture is rested on the three simple essentials of painting—pure Colour, noble Form, noble Thought.

We moderns, educated in reality far more under the influence of the Dutch masters than the Italian, and taught to look for realization in all things, have been in the habit of casting scorn on these early Italian works, as if their simplicity were the result of ignorance merely. When we know a little more of art in general, we shall begin to suspect that a man of Giotto's power of mind did not altogether suppose his clusters of formal trees, or diminutive masses of architecture, to be perfect representations of the woods of Judea, or of the streets of Jerusalem: we shall begin to understand that there is a symbolical art which addresses the imagination, as well as a realist art which supersedes it; and that the powers of contemplation and conception, which could be satisfied or excited by these simple types of natural things, were infinitely more majestic than those which are so dependent on the completeness of what is presented to them as to be paralysed by an error in perspective, or stifled by the absence of atmosphere.

24. Nor is the healthy simplicity of the period less marked in the selection than in the treatment of subjects. It has in these days become necessary for the painter who desires popularity to accumulate on his canvas whatever is startling in aspect or emotion, and to drain, even to exhaustion, the vulgar sources of the pathetic. Modern sentiment, at once feverish and feeble, remains unawakened except by the violences of gaiety or gloom; and the eye refuses to pause, except when it is tempted by the luxury of beauty, or fascinated by the excitement of terror. It ought not, therefore, to be without a respectful admiration that we find the masters of the fourteenth century dwelling on moments of the most subdued and tender feeling, and leaving the spectator to trace the undercurrents of thought which link them with future events of mightier interest, and fill with a prophetic power and mystery scenes in themselves so simple as the meeting of a master with his herdsmen among the hills, or the return of a betrothed virgin to her house.

It is, however, to be remembered that this quietness in character of subject was much more possible to an early painter, owing to the connection in which his works were to be seen. A modern picture, isolated and portable, must rest all its claims to attention on its own actual subject: but the pictures of the early masters were nearly always parts of a consecutive and stable series, in which many were subdued, like the connecting passages of a prolonged poem, in order to enhance the value or meaning of others. The arrangement of the subjects in the Arena Chapel is in this respect peculiarly skilful; and to that arrangement we must now direct our attention.

25. It was before noticed that the chapel was built between 1300 and 1306. The architecture of Italy in the beginning of the fourteenth century is always pure, and often severe; but this chapel is remarkable, even among the severest forms, for the absence of decoration. Its plan, seen in the marginal figure, is a pure oblong, with a narrow advanced tribune, terminating in a trilateral apse.[24] Selvatico quotes from the German writer Stieglitz some curious observations on the apparent derivation of its proportions, in common with those of other buildings of the time, from the number of sides of its apse. Without entering into these particulars, it may be noted that the apse is just one-half the width of the body of the chapel, and that the length from the extremity of the tribune to the west end is just seven times the width of the apse. The whole of the body of the chapel was painted by Giotto; the walls and roof being entirely covered either with his figure designs, or with various subordinate decorations connecting and enclosing them.

The woodcut opposite[25] represents the arrangement of the frescoes of the sides, extremities, and roof of the chapel. The spectator is supposed to be looking from the western entrance towards the tribune, having on his right the south side, which is pierced by six tall windows, and on which the frescoes are therefore reduced in number. The north side is pierced by no windows, and on it therefore the frescoes are continuous, lighted from the south windows. The several spaces numbered 1 to 38 are occupied by a continuous series of subjects, representing the life of the Virgin and of Christ; the narrow panels below, marked *a*, *b*, *c*, etc., are filled by figures of the cardinal virtues and their opponent vices; on the lunette above the tribune is painted a Christ in glory,[26] and at the western extremity, the Last Judgment. Thus the walls of the chapel are covered with a continuous meditative poem on the mystery of the Incarnation, the acts of Redemption, the vices and virtues of mankind as proceeding from their scorn or acceptance of that Redemption, and their final judgment.

The first twelve pictures of the series are exclusively devoted to the apocryphal history of the birth and life of the Virgin. This the Protestant spectator will observe, perhaps, with little favour, more especially as only two compartments are given to the ministry of Christ, between his Baptism and Entry into Jerusalem. Due weight is, however, to be allowed to Lord Lindsay's remark,[27] that the legendary history of the Virgin was of peculiar importance in this chapel, as especially dedicated to her

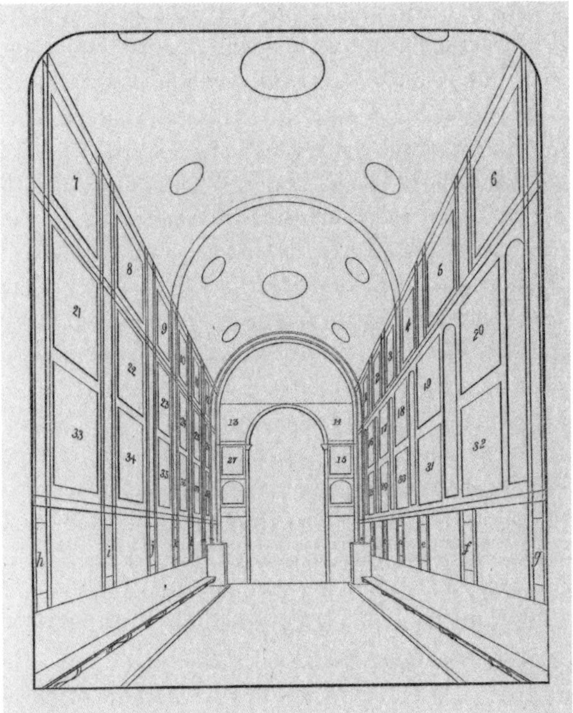

INTERIOR OF THE ARENA CHAPEL, PADUA, LOOKING EASTWARD.

A plan of the interior of the Scrovegni Chapel from the 1906 Cook-Wederburn Library Edition of *The Works of John Ruskin*.

service; and I think also that Giotto desired to unite the series of compositions in one continuous action, feeling that to have enlarged on the separate miracles of Christ's ministry would have interrupted the onward course of thought. As it is, the mind is led from the first humiliation of Joachim to the Ascension of Christ in one unbroken and progressive chain of scenes; the ministry of Christ being completely typified by his first and last conspicuous miracle: while the very unimportance of some of the subjects, as for instance that of the Watching of the Rods, is useful in directing the spectator rather to pursue the course of the narrative, than to pause in satisfied meditation upon any single incident. And it can hardly be doubted that Giotto had also a peculiar pleasure in dwelling on the circumstances of the shepherd life of the father of the Virgin, owing to its resemblance to that of his own early years.

26. The incidents represented in these first twelve paintings are recorded in the two apocryphal gospels known as the "Protevangelion" and "Gospel of St. Mary."[28] But on comparing the statements in these writings (which, by the bye, are in nowise consistent with each other) with the paintings in the Arena Chapel, it appeared to me that Giotto must occasionally have followed some more detailed traditions than are furnished by either of them; seeing that of one or two subjects the apocryphal gospels gave no distinct or sufficient explanation. Fortunately, however, in the course of some other researches, I met with a manuscript in the British Museum (Harl.

3571),[29] containing a complete "History of the most Holy Family," written in Northern Italian of about the middle of the fourteenth century; and appearing to be one of the forms of the legend which Giotto has occasionally followed in preference to the statements of the Protevangelion. I have therefore, in illustration of the paintings, given, when it seemed useful, some portions of this manuscript; and these, with one or two verses of the commonly received accounts, will be found generally enough to interpret sufficiently the meaning of the painter.

The following complete list of the subjects will at once enable the reader to refer any of them to its place in the series, and on the walls of the building; and I have only now to remind him in conclusion that within those walls the greatest painter and greatest poet of medieval Italy held happy companionship during the time when the frescoes were executed. "It is not difficult," says the writer already so often quoted, Lord Lindsay,[30] "gazing on these silent but eloquent walls, to repeople them with the group once, as we know, five hundred years ago, assembled within them: Giotto intent upon his work, his wife Ciuta admiring his progress; and Dante, with abstracted eye, alternately conversing with his friend, and watching the gambols of the children playing on the grass before the door."

1 Noting the visages of some who lay
Beneath the pelting of that dolorous fire,
One of them all I knew not; but perceived
That pendent from his neck each bore a pouch,
With colours and with emblems various marked,
On which it seemed as if their eye did feed.
And when amongst them looking round I came,
A yellow purse I saw, with azure wrought,
That wore a lion's countenance and port.
Then, still my sight pursuing its career,
Another I beheld, than blood more red,
A goose display of whiter wing than curd.
And one who bore a fat and azure srvine
Pictured on his white scrip, addressed me thus:
What dost thou in this deep? Go now and know,
Since yet thou livest, that my neighbour here,
Vitaliano, on my left shall sit.
A Paduan with these Florentines am I.
Ofttimes they thunder in mine ears, exclaiming,
Oh! haste that noble knight, he who the pouch
With the three goats will bring. This said, he writhed
The mouth, and lolled the tongue out, like an ox
That licks his nostrils.

—Canto 17

This passage of Cary's Dante is not quite so clear as that translator's work usually is. "One of them all I knew not" is an awkward periphrasis for "I knew none of them." Dante's indignant expression of the effect of avarice in withering away distinctions of character, and the prophecy of Scrovegno, that his neighbour Vitaliano, then living, should soon be with him, to sit on his left hand, is rendered a little obscure by the transposition of the word "here." Cary has also been afraid of the excessive homeliness of Dante's imagery; "whiter wing than curd" being in the original "whiter than butter." The attachment of the purse to the neck, as a badge of shame, in the *Inferno*, is found before Dante's time, as, for instance, in the windows of Bourges cathedral; see plate iii of MM. Martin and Cahier's beautiful work.[i] And the building of the Arena Chapel by the son, as a kind of atonement for the avarice of the father, is very characteristic of the period, in which the use of money for the building of churches was considered just as meritorious as its unjust accumulation was criminal. I have seen, in an MS church service of the thirteenth century, an illumination representing church consecration, illustrating the words "Fundata est domus Domini supra verticem montium,"[ii] surrounded, for the purpose of contrast, by a grotesque, consisting of a picture of a miser's deathbed, a demon drawing his soul out of his mouth, while his attendants are searching in his chests for his treasures.

i [Editor's note, 1906: Arthur Martin and Charles Cahier, *Monographie de la cathédrale de Bourges: Premiere partie, Vitraux du XIIIe siècle* (Paris: Poussielgue-Rusand, 1841–1844).]

ii [Ed. note, 2018: "The house of the Lord is fixed upon the mountain-top."]

2 For these historical details I am chiefly indebted to the very careful treatise of Selvatico, *Sulla Cappellina degli Scrovegni nell' Arena di Padova* (Padua: Tipi della Minerva, 1836).

3 [Ed. note, 1906: Robert Grosseteste (died 1253), Bishop of Lincoln; preached against papal abuses; suspended by the pope, 1251.]

4 [Ed. note, 1906: The date of Giotto's birth is still one of the unsettled questions of art history. The date of his work at the Arena Chapel (1305–1306) is fixed by early evidence, and bears upon the other question. Benvenuto Rambaldi da Imola (1331–1380) in his commentary upon Dante appends this note to the passage in which the poet refers to the eclipse of Cimabue's fame by Giotto: "Now it once happened that while Giotto, still fairly young, was painting at Padua a chapel in the place where was once the theatre or arena, Dante came to the place And Giotto received him with honour and took him to his house.... This Giotto lived afterwards for a long time, for he died in 1336." A Paduan record states that Dante was at Padua in 1306; see *Novelle Letterarie*, Florence, 1748, col. 361. A contemporary Florentine writer states that Giotto was seventy when he died: Antonio Pucci (died 1398) in his *Centiloquio*. If Giotto was born in 1276, he would have died at sixty; but if in 1266, he would have been forty when Benvenuto describes him as "adhuc satis juvenis."]

5 Lord Alexander Lindsay, *Sketches of the History of Christian Art*, vol. 2 (London: John Murray, 1847), p. 166.

6 At Pietra Mala. The flames rise two or three feet above the stony ground out of which they spring, white and fierce enough to be visible in the intense rays even of the morning sun.

7 At least Lord Lindsay seems to consider the evidence collected by Förster on this subject conclusive. Lindsay, *Christian Art*, vol. 2, p. 168.

8 [Ed. note, 1906: The Italian is "e girato la mano."]

9 [Ed. note, 1906: "Giotto had always a jest ready, and was never at a loss for a witty reply, so that he amused the king (of Naples) with his hand while he painted, and also by the acuteness of his pleasant conversation," etc. See Vasari, *Lives of the Artists*, vol. 1 (London: Henry Bohn, 1850), pp. 108, 119–121.]

10 It might not, I think, be a work unworthy of the Arundel Society, to collect and engrave in outline the complete series of these Byzantine originals

of the subjects of the Arena Chapel, in order to facilitate this comparison. The Greek MSS in the British Museum would, I think, be amply sufficient; the Harleian MS numbered 1810 alone furnishing a considerable number of subjects, and especially a Death of the Virgin, with the St. John thrown into the peculiar and violent gesture of grief afterwards adopted by Giotto in the Entombment of the Arena Chapel.

11 [Ed. note, 1906: Exodus 25:4.]

12 Note to Samuel Rogers, *Italy: A Poem* (London: Edward Moxon, 1839), p. 264.

13 [Ed. note, 1906: John 21:25.]

14 These words are gravely added to some singular particulars respecting the life of Adam, related in an MS of the sixteenth century preserved in the Heralds' College.

15 Lord Lindsay's evidence on this point (*Christian Art*, vol. 2, p. 174) seems quite conclusive. It is impossible to overrate the value of the work of Giotto in the Bargello, both for its own intrinsic beauty, and as being executed in this year, which is not only that in which the *Divina Commedia* opens, but, as I think, the culminating period in the history of the art of the Middle Ages.

16 [Ed. note, 1906: Here Ruskin follows Lord Lindsay (*Christian Art*, vol. 2, pp. 124–125) into error. Arnolfo did not die till 1310, and the work upon the cathedral stopped till 1334, when (as a document of 12 April in that year attests) Giotto (as Ruskin says lower down) was appointed by public decree Capo-Maestro of the cathedral and architect of the Commune. Tradition records that he then commenced the decoration of the old façade, which, however, was never completed; and then, too, he designed, and executed some part of, the Campanile. The account in the text of Giotto's other movements must also be taken with some reserve.]

17 Lindsay, *Christian Art*, vol. 2, p. 242.

18 [Ed. note, 1906: Lindsay, *Christian Art*, vol. 2, pp. 244, 246.]

19 [Ed. note, 1906: i.e., in the old style; 1336 in our method of reckoning.]

20 [Ed. note, 1906: Deuteronomy 34:7.]

21 Lindsay, *Christian Art*, vol. 2, p. 260.

22 [Ed. note, 1906: Here, again, Ruskin follows Lord Lindsay (*Christian Art*, vol. 2, pp. 244, 245) into error. There are no works by Giotto remaining at Naples. The frescoes in the Church of l'Incoronata, once extolled as his, cannot be so, for it has been ascertained that the first stone of the building was not laid till some years after Giotto's death.]

23 I use this heraldic word in an inaccurate sense, knowing no other that will express what I mean—the division of the picture into quaint segments of alternating colour, more marked than any of the figure outlines.

24 [Ed. note, 2018: This illustration was originally reproduced as a marginal figure.]

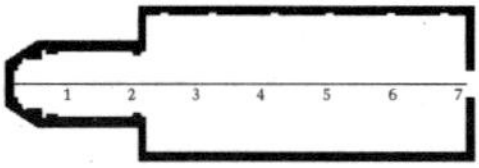

25 [Ed. note, 1906: Redrawn and made clearer in this edition.]

26 [Ed. note, 2018: Ruskin and his contemporaries believed that the fresco on the arch above the altar consisted of two parts: Christ in glory on the upper lunette and the Annunciation on the two smaller panels below it. It is now commonly accepted that the fresco depicts God sending the archangel Gabriel to tell Mary she will give birth to Jesus, so that the entire arch forms the story of the Annunciation.]

27 [Ed. note, 1906: Lindsay, *Christian Art*, vol. 2, p. 184.]

28 It has always appeared strange to me that ecclesiastical history should possess no more authentic records of the life of the Virgin, before the period at which the narrative of St. Luke commences, than these apocryphal gospels,[i] which are as wretched in style as untrustworthy in matter; and are evidently nothing more than a collection, in rude imitation of the style of the Evangelists, of such floating traditions as became current among the weak Christians of the earlier ages, when their inquiries respecting the history of Mary were met by the obscurity under which the Divine will had veiled her humble person and character. There must always be something painful, to those who are familiar with the Scriptures, in reading these feeble and foolish mockeries of the manner of the inspired writers; but it will be proper, nevertheless, to give the exact words in which the scenes represented by Giotto were recorded to *him*.

i [Ed. note, 1906: The "Protevangel of James" was a narrative extending from the Conception of the Virgin to the Death of Zacharias; it is supposed to belong to the first decade of the second century. The critics distinguish between (*a*) an original Jewish Christian writing, and (*b*) a Gnostic recast of it. From (*a*) arose the *Protevangel* in its present form (Greek); from (*b*), a Latin pseudo-Matthaeus, of which the *Evangelium de Nativitate Mariæ* (referred to by Ruskin as "The Gospel of St. Mary") is a redaction.]

29 [Ed. note, 1906: Thus described in the Catalogue of MSS: "*La vita de Joachy, e Anna, e Maria, e Yesu Christo*. An Italian Legendary History of the Holy Family, illuminated throughout, but in a very coarse style. On vellum."]

30 [Ed. note, 1906: Lindsay, *Christian Art*, vol. 2, p. 199.]

I
The Rejection of Joachim's Offering

"At that time, there was a man of perfect holiness, named Joachim, of the tribe of Juda, and of the city of Jerusalem. And this Joachim had in contempt the riches and honours of the world; and for greater despite to them, he kept his flocks, with his shepherds.

"... And he, being so holy and just, divided the fruits which he received from his flocks into three parts: a third part—wool, and lambs, and suchlike—he gave to God, that is to say, to those who served God, and who ministered in the temple of God; another third part he gave to widows, orphans, and pilgrims; the remaining third he kept for himself and his family. And he persevering in this, God so multiplied and increased his goods that there was no man like him in the land of Israel.... And having come to the age of twenty years, he took to wife Anna, the daughter of Ysaya, of his own tribe, and of the lineage of David.

"This precious St. Anna had always persevered in the service of God with great wisdom and sincerity... and having received Joachim for her husband, was subject to him, and gave him honour and reverence, living in the fear of God. And Joachim having lived with his wife Anna for twenty years, yet having no child, and there being a great solemnity in Jerusalem, all the men of the city went to offer in the temple of God, which Solomon had built; and Joachim entering the temple with (incense?) and other gifts to offer on the altar, and Joachim having made his offering, the minister of the temple, whose name was Issachar, threw Joachim's offering from off the altar, and drove Joachim out of the temple, saying, 'Thou, Joachim, art not worthy to enter into the temple, seeing that God has not added His blessing to you, as in your life you have had no seed.' Thus Joachim received a great insult in the sight of all the people; and he being all ashamed, returned to his house, weeping and lamenting most bitterly." (MS Harl.)

The Gospel of St. Mary differs from this MS in its statement of the respective cities of Joachim and Anna, saying that the family of the Virgin's father "was of Galilee and of the city of Nazareth, the family of her mother was of Bethlehem." It is less interesting in details; but gives a better, or at least more graceful, account of Joachim's repulse, saying that Issachar "despised Joachim and his offerings, and asked him why he, who had no children, would presume to appear among those who had: adding that his offerings could never be acceptable to God, since he had been judged by Him unworthy to have children; the Scripture having said, Cursed is every one who shall not beget a male in Israel."[1]

Giotto seems to have followed this latter account, as the figure of the high priest is far from being either ignoble or ungentle.

The temple is represented by the two most important portions of a Byzantine church; namely, the ciborium which covered the altar, and the pulpit or reading desk;

with the low screen in front of the altar enclosing the part of the church called the "cancellum." Lord Lindsay speaks of the priest within this enclosure as "confessing a young man who kneels at his feet."[2] It seems to me, rather, that he is meant to be accepting the offering of another worshipper, so as to mark the rejection of Joachim more distinctly.

1 [Ed. note, 1906: Gospel of St. Mary 1:8–9.]
2 [Ed. note, 1906: Lindsay, *Christian Art*, vol. 2, p. 186.]

11
Joachim Retires to the Sheepfold

"Then Joachim, in the following night, resolved to separate himself from companionship; to go to the desert places among the mountains, with his flocks; and to inhabit those mountains, in order not to hear such insults. And immediately Joachim rose from his bed, and called about him all his servants and shepherds, and caused to be gathered together all his flocks, and goats, and horses, and oxen, and what other beasts he had, and went with them and with the shepherds into the hills; and Anna his wife remained at home disconsolate, and mourning for her husband, who had departed from her in such sorrow." (MS Harl.)

"But upon inquiry, he found that all the righteous had raised up seed in Israel. Then he called to mind the patriarch Abraham—how that God in the end of his life had given him his son Isaac: upon which he was exceedingly distressed, and would not be seen by his wife; but retired into the wilderness and fixed his tent there, and fasted forty days and forty nights, saying to himself, 'I will not go down to eat or drink till the Lord my God shall look down upon me; but prayer shall be my meat and drink.'" (Protevangelion 1:4–7.)

Giotto seems here also to have followed the ordinary tradition, as he has represented Joachim retiring unattended—but met by two of his shepherds, who are speaking to each other, uncertain what to do or how to receive their master. The dog hastens to meet him with joy. The figure of Joachim is singularly beautiful in its pensiveness and slow motion; and the ignobleness of the herdsmen's figures is curiously marked in opposition to the dignity of their master.

III
The Angel Appears to Anna

"Afterwards the angel appeared to Anna his wife, saying, 'Fear not, neither think that which you see is a spirit. For I am that angel who hath offered up your prayers and alms before God, and am now sent to tell you that a daughter will be born unto you.... Arise, therefore, and go up to Jerusalem; and when you shall come to that which is called the Golden Gate (because it is gilt with gold), as a sign of what I have told you, you shall meet your husband, for whose safety you have been so much concerned.'" (Gospel of St. Mary 3:1–2, 6.)

The accounts in the Protevangelion and in the Harleian MS are much expanded: relating how Anna feared her husband was dead, he having been absent from her five months; and how Judith, her maid, taunted her with her childlessness; and how, going then into her garden, she saw a sparrow's nest, full of young, upon a laurel tree, and mourning within herself said, "'I am not comparable to the very beasts of the earth, for even they are fruitful before Thee, O Lord.... I am not comparable to the very earth, for the earth produces its fruits to praise Thee.' Then the angel of the Lord stood by her," etc.

Both the Protevangelion and Harleian MS agree in placing the vision in the garden; the latter adding that she fled "into her chamber in great fear, and fell upon her bed, and lay as in a trance all that day and all that night, but did not tell the vision to her maid, because of her bitter answering." Giotto has deviated from both accounts in making the vision appear to Anna in her chamber, while the maid, evidently being considered an important personage, is at work in the passage. Apart from all reference to the legends, there is something peculiarly beautiful in the simplicity of Giotto's conception, and in the way in which he has shown the angel entering at the window, without the least endeavour to impress our imagination by darkness, or light, or clouds, or any other accessory; as though believing that angels might appear anywhere, and any day, and to all men, as a matter of course, if we would ask them, or were fit company for them.

IV
The Sacrifice of Joachim

The account of this sacrifice is only given clearly in the Harleian MS; but even this differs from Giotto's series in the order of the visions, as the subject of the *next* plate is recorded first in this MS, under the curious heading, "*Disse Sancto Theofilo* como l'angelo de Dio aperse a Joachim lo qual li anuntia la nativita della vergene Maria"; while the record of this vision and sacrifice is headed, "Como l'angelo de Dio aparse *anchora* a Joachim." It then proceeds thus: "At this very moment of the day" (when the angel appeared to Anna), "there appeared a most beautiful youth (*unno belitissimo zovene*) among the mountains there, where Joachim was, and said to Joachim, 'Wherefore dost thou not return to thy wife?' And Joachim answered, 'These twenty years God has given me no fruit of her, wherefore I was chased from the temple with infinite shame.... And, as long as I live, I will give alms of my flocks to widows and pilgrims.' ... And these words being finished, the youth answered, 'I am the angel of God who appeared to thee the other time for a sign; and appeared to thy wife Anna, who always abides in prayer, weeping day and night; and I have consoled her; wherefore I command thee to observe the commandments of God, and His will, which I tell you truly, that of thee shall be born a daughter, and that thou shalt offer her to the temple of God, and the Holy Spirit shall rest upon her, and her blessedness shall be above the blessedness of all virgins, and her holiness so great that human nature will not be able to comprehend it.'[1] . . .

"Then Joachim fell upon the earth, saying, 'My lord, I pray thee to pray God for me, and to enter into this my tabernacle, and bless me, thy servant.' The angel answered, 'We are all the servants of God: and know that my eating would be invisible, and my drinking could not be seen by all the men in the world; but of all that thou wouldest give to me, do thou make sacrifice to God.' Then Joachim took a lamb without spot or blemish . . . and when he had made sacrifice of it, the angel of the Lord disappeared and ascended into heaven; and Joachim fell upon the earth in great fear, and lay from the sixth hour until the evening."

This is evidently nothing more than a very vapid imitation of the scriptural narrative of the appearances of angels to Abraham and Manoah. But Giotto has put life into it; and I am aware of no other composition in which so much interest and awe has been given to the literal "burnt sacrifice." In all other representations of such offerings which I remember, the interest is concentrated in the *slaying* of the victim. But Giotto has fastened on the *burning* of it; showing the white skeleton left on the altar, and the fire still hurtling up round it, typical of the Divine wrath, which is "as a consuming fire";[2] and thus rendering the sacrifice a more clear and fearful type not merely of the outward wounds and death of Christ, but of His soul-suffering. "All my bones are out of joint:[3] my heart is like wax; it is melted in the midst of my bowels."[4]

The hand of the Deity is seen in the heavens—the sign of the Divine Presence.

1 This passage in the old Italian of the MS may interest some readers: "E complice queste parole lo zovene respoxe, dignando, Io son l'angelo de Dio, lo quale si te aparse l'altra fiada, in segno, e aparse a toa mulier Anna che sempre sta in oration plauzando di e note, e si lo consolada; unde io te comando che tu debie observare li comandimenti de Dio, ela soua volunta che io te dico veramente, che de la toa somenza insera una fioils, e questa offrila al templo de Dio, e lo Spirito santo reposera in ley, ela soa beatitudine sera sovera tute le altre verzene, ela soua santita sera si grande che natura humana non la pora comprendere."

2 [Ed. note, 1906: Deuteronomy 4:24.]

3 [Ed. note, 1906: Psalms 22:14.]

4 (Note by a friend.) "To me the most striking part of it is that the skeleton is *entire* ('a bone of him shall not be broken'), and that the head stands up still looking to the skies: is it too fanciful to see a meaning in this?"

V

The Angel (Raphael) Appears to Joachim

"Now Joachim being in this pain, the Lord God, Father of mercy, who abandons not His servants, nor ever fails to console them in their distresses, if they pray for His grace and pity, had compassion on Joachim, and heard his prayer, and sent the angel Raphael from heaven to earth to console him, and announce to him the nativity of the Virgin Mary. Therefore the angel Raphael appeared to Joachim, and comforted him with much peace, and foretold to him the birth of the Virgin in that glory and gladness, saying, 'God save you, O friend of God, O Joachim! the Lord has sent me to declare to you an everlasting joy, and a hope that shall have no end.' . . . And having finished these words, the angel of the Lord disappeared from him, and ascended into the heaven." (MS Harl.)

The passage which I have omitted is merely one of the ordinary Romanist accounts of the immaculate conception of the Virgin, put into the form of prophecy. There are no sufficient details of this part of the legend either in the Protevangelion or Gospel of St. Mary; but it is quite clear that Giotto followed it, and that he has endeavoured to mark a distinction in character between the angels Gabriel and Raphael[1] in the two subjects—the form of Raphael melting back into the heaven, and being distinctly recognized as angelic, while Gabriel appears invested with perfect humanity. It is interesting to observe that the shepherds, who of course are not supposed to see the form of the Angel (his manifestation being only granted to Joachim during his sleep), are yet evidently under the influence of a certain degree of awe and expectation, as being conscious of some presence other than they can perceive, while the animals are unconscious altogether.

1 The MS makes the angel Raphael the only messenger. Giotto clearly adopts the figure of Gabriel from the Protevangelion.

VI

The Meeting at the Golden Gate

"And Joachim went down with the shepherds, and Anna stood by the gate, and saw Joachim coming with the shepherds. And she ran, and hanging about his neck, said, 'Now I know that the Lord hath greatly blessed me.'" (Protevangelion 4:8–9.)

This is one of the most celebrated of Giotto's compositions, and deservedly so, being full of the most solemn grace and tenderness. The face of St. Anna, half seen, is most touching in its depth of expression; and it is very interesting to observe how Giotto has enhanced its sweetness, by giving a harder and grosser character than is usual with him to the heads of the other two principal female figures (not but that this cast of feature is found frequently in the figures of somewhat earlier art), and by the rough and weather-beaten countenance of the entering shepherd. In like manner, the falling lines of the draperies owe a great part of their value to the abrupt and ugly oblongs of the horizontal masonry which adjoins them.

VII
The Birth of the Virgin

"And Joachim said, 'Now I know that the Lord is propitious to me, and hath taken away all my sins.' And he went down from the temple of the Lord justified, and went to his own house.

"And when nine months were fulfilled to Anna, she brought forth, and said to the midwife, 'What have I brought forth?' And she told her, a girl.

"Then Anna said, 'The Lord hath this day magnified my soul.' And she laid her in the bed." (Protevangelion 5:4–8.)

The composition is very characteristic of Giotto in two respects: first, in its natural homeliness and simplicity (in older designs of the same subject the little Madonna is represented as born with a golden crown on her head); and secondly, in the smallness of the breast and head of the sitting figure on the right—a fault of proportion often observable in Giotto's figures of children or young girls.

For the first time, also, in this series, we have here two successive periods of the scene represented simultaneously, the babe being painted twice. This practice was frequent among the early painters, and must necessarily become so wherever painting undertakes the task of lengthened narrative. Much absurd discussion has taken place respecting its propriety; the whole question being simply whether the human mind can or cannot pass from the contemplation of one event to that of another, without reposing itself on an intermediate gilt frame.

VIII
The Presentation of the Virgin

"And when three years were expired, and the time of her weaning complete, they brought the Virgin to the temple of the Lord with offerings.

"And there were about the temple, according to the fifteen Psalms of Degrees, fifteen stairs to ascend.

"The parents of the blessed Virgin and infant Mary put her upon one of these stairs; but while they were putting off their clothes in which they had travelled, in the meantime, the Virgin of the Lord in such a manner went up all the stairs, one after another, without the help of anyone to lead her or lift her, that anyone would have judged from hence that she was of perfect age." (Gospel of St. Mary 4:1–6.)

There seems nothing very miraculous in a child's walking up stairs at three years old; but this incident is a favourite one among the Roman Catholic painters of every period: generally, however, representing the child as older than in the legend, and dwelling rather on the solemn feeling with which she presents herself to the high priest, than on the mere fact of her being able to walk alone. Giotto has clearly regarded the incident entirely in this light, for St. Anna touches the child's arm as if to support her, so that the so-called miraculous walking is not even hinted at.

Lord Lindsay particularly notices that the Virgin is "a dwarf woman instead of a child—the delineation of childhood was one of the latest triumphs of art."[1] Even in the time of those latest triumphs, however, the same fault was committed in another way; and a boy of eight or ten was commonly represented—even by Raphael himself—as a dwarf Hercules, with all the gladiatorial muscles already visible in stunted rotundity. Giotto probably felt he had not power enough to give dignity to a child of three years old, and intended the womanly form to be rather typical of the Virgin's advanced mind, than an actual representation of her person.

1 [Ed. note, 1906: Lindsay, *Christian Art*, vol. 2, p. 187.]

IX
The Rods Are Brought to the High Priest

"Then he (the high priest) appointed that all the men of the house and family of David who were marriageable, and not married, should bring their several rods to the altar. And out of whatsoever person's rod, after it was brought, a flower should bud forth, and on the top of it the Spirit of the Lord should sit in the appearance of a dove, he should be the man to whom the Virgin should be given, and be betrothed to her." (Gospel of St. Mary 5:16–17.)

There has originally been very little interest in this composition; and the injuries which it has suffered have rendered it impossible for the draughtsman to distinguish the true folds of the draperies amidst the defaced and worn colours of the fresco, so that the character of the central figure is lost. The only points requiring notice are, first, the manner in which St. Joseph holds his rod, depressing and half concealing it,[1] while the other suitors present theirs boldly; and secondly, the graceful though monotonous grouping of the heads of the crowd behind him. This mode of rendering the presence of a large multitude, showing only the crowns of the heads in complicated perspective, was long practised in mosaics and illuminations before the time of Giotto, and always possesses a certain degree of sublimity in its power of suggesting perfect unity of feeling and movement among the crowd.

1 In the next chapter it is said that "Joseph drew back his rod when every one else presented his."

X
The Watching of the Rods at the Altar

"After the high priest had received their rods, he went into the temple to pray.

"And when he had finished his prayer, he took the rods and went forth and distributed them; and there was no miracle attended them.

"The last rod was taken by Joseph; and behold, a dove proceeded out of the rod, and flew upon the head of Joseph." (Protevangelion 8:9–11.)

This is among the least graceful designs of the series; though the clumsiness in the contours of the leading figures is indeed a fault which often occurs in the painter's best works, but it is here unredeemed by the rest of the composition. The group of the suitors, however, represented as waiting at the outside of the temple, is very beautiful in its earnestness, more especially in the passionate expression of the figure in front. It is difficult to look long at the picture without feeling a degree of anxiety, and strong sympathy with the silent watching of the suitors; and this is a sign of no small power in the work. The head of Joseph is seen far back on the extreme left; thus indicating by its position his humility, and desire to withdraw from the trial.

XI

The Betrothal of the Virgin

There is no distinct notice of this event in the apocryphal Gospel: the traditional representation of it is nearly always more or less similar. Lord Lindsay's account of the composition before us is as follows:

"The high priest, standing in front of the altar, joins their hands; behind the Virgin stand her bridesmaids; behind St. Joseph the unsuccessful suitors, one of whom steps forward to strike him, and another breaks his rod on his knee. Joseph bears his own rod, on the flower of which the Holy Spirit rests in the semblance of a dove."[1]

The development of this subject by Perugino (for Raphael's picture in the Brera is little more than a modified copy of Perugino's, now at Caen) is well known; but notwithstanding all its beauty, there is not, I think, anything in the action of the disappointed suitors so perfectly true or touching as that of the youth breaking his rod in this composition of Giotto's; nor is there among any of the figures the expression of solemn earnestness and intentness on the event which is marked among the attendants here, and in the countenances of the officiating priests.

1 [Ed. note, 1906: Lindsay, *Christian Art*, vol. 2, p. 187.]

XII
The Virgin Mary Returns to Her House

"Accordingly, the usual ceremonies of betrothing being over, he (Joseph) returned to his own city of Bethlehem to set his house in order, and to make the needful provisions for the marriage. But the Virgin of the Lord, Mary, with seven other virgins of the same age, who had been weaned at the same time, and who had been appointed to attend her by the priest, returned to her parents' house in Galilee." (Gospel of St. Mary 6:6–7.)

Of all the compositions in the Arena Chapel I think this the most characteristic of the noble time in which it was done. It is not so notable as exhibiting the mind of Giotto, which is perhaps more fully seen in subjects representing varied emotion, as in the simplicity and repose which were peculiar to the compositions of the early fourteenth century. In order to judge of it fairly, it ought first to be compared with any classical composition—with a portion, for instance, of the Elgin frieze—which would instantly make manifest in it a strange seriousness and dignity and slowness of motion, resulting chiefly from the excessive simplicity of all its terminal lines. Observe, for instance, the pure wave from the back of the Virgin's head to the ground; and again, the delicate swelling line along her shoulder and left arm, opposed to the nearly unbroken fall of the drapery of the figure in front. It should then be compared with an Egyptian or Ninevite series of figures, which, by contrast, would bring out its perfect sweetness and grace, as well as its variety of expression: finally, it should be compared with any composition subsequent to the time of Raphael, in order to feel its noble freedom from pictorial artifice and attitude. These three comparisons cannot be made carefully without a sense of profound reverence for the national spirit[1] which could produce a design so majestic, and yet remain content with one so simple.

The small *loggia* of the Virgin's house is noticeable, as being different from the architecture introduced in the other pictures, and more accurately representing the Italian Gothic of the dwelling house of the period. The arches of the windows have no capitals; but this omission is either to save time, or to prevent the background from becoming too conspicuous. All the real buildings designed by Giotto have the capital completely developed.

1 *National*, because Giotto's works are properly to be looked on as the *fruit* of their own age, and the *food* of that which followed.

XIII
The Annunciation—The Angel Gabriel

This figure is placed on one side of the arch at the east end of the body of the chapel; the corresponding figure of the Virgin being set on the other side. It was a constant practice of the medieval artists thus to divide this subject; which, indeed, was so often painted, that the meaning of the separated figures of the Angel and Mary was as well understood as when they were seen in juxtaposition. Indeed, on the two sides of this arch they would hardly be considered as separated, since very frequently they were set to answer to each other from the opposite extremities of a large space of architecture.[1]

The figure of the Angel is notable chiefly for its serenity, as opposed to the later conceptions of the scene, in which he falls into the chamber upon the wing, like a stooping falcon.

The building above is more developed than in any other of the Arena paintings; but it must always remain a matter of question, why so exquisite a designer of architecture as Giotto should introduce forms so harsh and meagre into his backgrounds. Possibly he felt that the very faults of the architecture enhanced the grace and increased the importance of the figures; at least, the proceeding seems to me inexplicable on any other theory.[2]

1 As, for instance, on the two opposite angles of the façade of the Cathedral of Rheims.

2 (Note by a friend.) "I suppose you will not admit as an explanation that he had not yet turned his mind to architectural composition, the Campanile being some thirty years later?"

XIV
The Annunciation—The Virgin Mary

Vasari, in his notice of one of Giotto's Annunciations, praises him for having justly rendered the *fear* of the Virgin at the address of the Angel. If he ever treated the subject in such a manner, he departed from all the traditions of his time; for I am aware of no painting of this scene, during the course of the thirteenth and following centuries, which does not represent the Virgin as perfectly tranquil, receiving the message of the Angel in solemn thought and gentle humility, but without a shadow of fear. It was reserved for the painters of the sixteenth and seventeenth centuries to change angelic majesty into reckless impetuosity, and maiden meditation[1] into panic dread.

The face of the Virgin is slightly disappointing. Giotto never reached a very high standard of beauty in feature; depending much on distant effect in all his works, and therefore more on general arrangement of colour and sincerity of gesture, than on refinement of drawing in the countenance.

1 [Ed. note, 1906: Shakespeare, *A Midsummer Night's Dream*, act 2, scene 1.]

XV
The Salutation

This picture, placed beneath the figure of the Virgin Annunciate at the east end of the chapel, and necessarily small (as will be seen by the plan) in consequence of the space occupied by the arch which it flanks, begins the second or lower series of frescoes; being, at the same time, the first of the great chain of more familiar subjects, in which we have the power of comparing the conceptions of Giotto not only with the designs of earlier ages, but with the efforts which subsequent masters have made to exalt or vary the ideas of the principal scenes in the life of the Virgin and of Christ. The two paintings of the Angel Gabriel and the Virgin Annunciate hardly provoke such a comparison, being almost statue-like in the calm subjection of all dramatic interest to the symmetrical dignity and beauty of the two figures, leading, as they do, the whole system of the decoration of the chapel; but this of the Salutation is treated with no such reference to the architecture, and at once challenges comparison with the works of later masters.

Nor is the challenge feebly maintained. I have no hesitation in saying that among all the renderings of this scene which now exist, I remember none which gives the pure depth and plain facts of it so perfectly as this of Giotto's. Of majestic women bowing themselves to beautiful and meek girls, both wearing gorgeous robes, in the midst of lovely scenery, or at the doors of

Palladian palaces, we have enough; but I do not know any picture which seems to me to give so truthful an idea of the action with which Elizabeth and Mary must actually have met—which gives so exactly the way in which Elizabeth would stretch her arms, and stoop and gaze into Mary's face, and the way in which Mary's hand would slip beneath Elizabeth's arms, and raise her up to kiss her. I know not any Elizabeth so full of intense love, and joy, and humbleness; hardly any Madonna in which tenderness and dignity are so quietly blended. She not less humble, and yet accepting the reverence of Elizabeth as her appointed portion, saying, in her simplicity and truth, "He that is mighty hath magnified me, and holy is His name." The longer that this group is looked upon, the more it will be felt that Giotto has done well to withdraw from it nearly all accessories of landscape and adornment, and to trust it to the power of its own deep expression. We may gaze upon the two silent figures until their silence seems to be broken, and the words of the question and reply sound in our ears, low, as if from far away:

"Whence is this to me that the Mother of my Lord should come to me?"

"My soul doth magnify the Lord, and my spirit hath rejoiced in God my Saviour."[1]

1 [Ed. note, 1906: Luke 1:49, 43, 46–47.]

XVI
The Nativity

I am not sure whether I shall do well or kindly in telling the reader anything about this beautiful design. Perhaps the less he knows about early art or early traditions, the more deeply he will feel its purity and truth; for there is scarcely an incident here, or anything in the manner of representing the incidents, which is not mentioned or justified in Scripture. The bold hilly background reminds us that Bethlehem was in the hill country of Judah. But it may seem to have two purposes besides this literal one: the first, that it increases the idea of *exposure* and loneliness in the birth of Christ; the second, that the masses of the great hills, with the angels floating round them in the horizontal clouds, may in some sort represent to our thoughts the power and space of that heaven and earth whose Lord is being laid in the manger cradle.

There is an exquisite truth and sweetness in the way the Virgin turns upon the couch, in order herself to assist in laying the Child down. Giotto is in this exactly faithful to the scriptural words: "*She* wrapped the Child in swaddling clothes, and *laid* Him in a manger."[1] Joseph sits beneath in meditation; above, the angels, all exulting, and, as it were, confused with joy, flutter and circle in the air like birds—three looking up to the Father's throne with praise and thankfulness, one stooping to adore the Prince of Peace, one flying to tell the shepherds. There is something to me peculiarly affecting in this disorder of theirs; even angels, as it were, breaking their ranks with wonder, and not knowing how to utter their gladness and passion of praise. There is noticeable here, as in all works of this early time, a certain confidence in the way in which the angels trust to their wings, very characteristic of a period of bold and simple conception. Modern science has taught us that a wing cannot be anatomically joined to a shoulder; and in proportion as painters approach more and more to the scientific, as distinguished from the contemplative state of mind, they put the wings of their angels on more timidly, and dwell with greater emphasis upon the human form, and with less upon the wings, until these last become a species of decorative appendage—a mere *sign* of an angel. But in Giotto's time an angel was a complete creature, as much believed in as a bird; and the way in which it would or might cast itself into the air, and lean hither and thither upon its plumes, was as naturally apprehended as the manner of flight of a chough or a starling. Hence Dante's simple and most exquisite synonym for angel, "Bird of God";[2] and hence also a variety and picturesqueness in the expression of the movements of the heavenly hierarchies by the earlier painters, ill replaced by the powers of foreshortening, and throwing naked limbs into fantastic positions, which appear in the cherubic groups of later times.

It is needless to point out the frank association of the two events—the Nativity, and appearance of the Angel to the Shepherds. They are constantly thus joined; but I do not remember any other example in which they are joined so boldly. Usually the shepherds are seen in the distance, or are introduced in some ornamental border, or other inferior place. The view of painting as a mode of suggesting relative or consecutive thoughts, rather than a realization of any one scene, is seldom so fearlessly asserted, even by Giotto, as here, in placing the flocks of the shepherds at the foot of the Virgin's bed.

This bed, it will be noticed, is on a shelf of rock. This is in compliance with the idea founded on the Protevangelion and the apocryphal book known as the Gospel of Infancy,[3] that our Saviour was born in a cave, associated with the scriptural statement that He was laid in a manger, of which the apocryphal gospels do not speak.

The vain endeavour to exalt the awe of the moment of the Saviour's birth has turned, in these gospels, the outhouse of the inn into a species of subterranean chapel, full of incense and candles. "It was after sunset, when the old woman (the midwife), and Joseph with her, reached the cave; and they both went into it. And behold, it was all filled with light, greater than the light of lamps and candles, and greater than the light of the sun itself." (Infancy 1:9.) "Then a bright cloud overshadowed the cave, and the midwife said: This day my soul is magnified." (Protevangelion 14:10.) The thirteenth chapter of the Protevangelion is, however, a little more skilful in this attempt at exaltation. "And leaving her and his sons in the cave, Joseph went forth to seek a Hebrew midwife in the village of Bethlehem. But as I was going, said Joseph,

I looked up into the air, and I saw the clouds astonished, and the fowls of the air stopping in the midst of their flight. And I looked down towards the earth and saw a table spread, and working people sitting around it; but their hands were on the table, and they did not move to eat. But all their faces were fixed upwards." (Protevangelion 13:1–3, 7.)

It would, of course, be absurd to endeavour to institute any comparison between the various pictures of this subject, innumerable as they are; but I must at least deprecate Lord Lindsay's characterizing this design of Giotto's merely as the "Byzantine composition."[4] It contains, indeed, nothing more than the materials of the Byzantine composition; but I know no Byzantine Nativity which at all resembles it in the grace and life of its action. And, for full a century after Giotto's time, in Northern Europe, the Nativity was represented in a far more conventional manner than this—usually only the heads of the ox and ass are seen, and they are arranging, or holding with their mouths, the drapery of the couch of the Child, who is not being laid in it by the Virgin, but raised upon a kind of tablet high above her in the centre of the group. All these early designs, without exception, however, agree in expressing a certain degree of languor in the figure of the Virgin, and in making her recumbent on the bed. It is not till the fifteenth century that she is represented as exempt from suffering, and immediately kneeling in adoration before the Child.

1 [Ed. note, 1906: Luke 2:7.]

2 [Ed. note, 1906: Dante, *Purgatorio*, canto 2, line 38: "L'uccel divino."]

3 [Ed. note, 1906: "*The Arabic Gospel of the Childhood* (*Evangelium Infantiæ Arabicum*) is a Catholic recension of all the stories of the childhood from the birth of Jesus till His twelfth year. It is a special favourite with the Nestorians of Syria." William Smith and Henry Wace, *A Dictionary of Christian Biography, Literature, Sects and Doctrines*, vol. 2 (London: John Murray, 1890), p. 705.]

4 [Ed. note, 1906: Lindsay, *Christian Art*, vol. 2, p. 188.]

XVII

The Wise Men's Offering

This is a subject which has been so great a favourite with the painters of later periods, and on which so much rich incidental invention has been lavished, that Giotto's rendering of it cannot but be felt to be barren. It is, in fact, perhaps the least powerful of all the series; and its effect is further marred by what Lord Lindsay has partly noted,[1] the appearance—perhaps accidental, but if so, exceedingly unskilful—of matronly corpulence in the figure of the Madonna. The unfortunate failure in the representation of the legs and chests of the camels, and the awkwardness of the attempt to render the action of kneeling in the foremost king, put the whole composition into the class—not in itself an uninteresting one—of the slips or shortcomings of great masters. One incident in it only is worth observing. In other compositions of this time, and in many later ones, the kings are generally presenting their offerings themselves, and the Child takes them in His hand, or smiles at them. The painters who thought this an undignified conception left the presents in the hands of the attendants of the Magi. But Giotto considers how presents would be received by an actual king; and as what has been offered to a monarch is delivered to the care of his attendants, Giotto puts a waiting angel to receive the gifts, as not worthy to be placed in the hands of the Infant.

1 [Ed. note, 1906: "Her face sweet, though she is too matronly in form" (Lindsay, *Christian Art*, vol. 2, p. 188).]

XVIII

The Presentation in the Temple

This design is one of those which are peculiarly characteristic of Giotto as the head of the Naturalisti.[1] No painter before his time would have dared to represent the Child Jesus as desiring to quit the arms of Simeon, or the Virgin as in some sort interfering with the prophet's earnest contemplation of the Child by stretching her arms to receive Him. The idea is evidently a false one, quite unworthy of the higher painters of the religious school; and it is a matter of peculiar interest to see what must have been the strength of Giotto's love of plain facts, which could force him to stoop so low in the conception of this most touching scene. The child does not, it will be observed, merely stretch its arm to the Madonna, but is even struggling to escape, violently raising the left foot. But there is another incident in the composition, witnessing as notably to Giotto's powerful grasp of all the facts of his subject as this does to his somewhat hard and plain manner of grasping them—I mean the angel approaching Simeon, as if with a message. The peculiar interest of the Presentation is for the most part inadequately represented in painting, because it is impossible to imply the fact of Simeon's having waited so long in the hope of beholding his Lord, or to inform the spectator of the feeling in which he utters the song of hope fulfilled. Giotto has, it seems to me, done all that he could to make us remember this peculiar meaning of the scene; for I think I cannot be deceived in interpreting the flying angel, with its branch of palm or lily, to be the Angel of Death, sent in visible fulfilment of the thankful words of Simeon: "Lord, now lettest Thou Thy servant depart in peace."[2] The figure of Anna is poor and uninteresting; that of the attendant, on the extreme left, very beautiful, both in its drapery and in the severe and elevated character of the features and headdress.

1 See account of his principles above, p. 39, § 12 (C).
2 [Ed. note, 1906: Luke 2:29.]

XIX
The Flight into Egypt

Giotto again shows, in his treatment of this subject, a juster understanding of the probable facts than most other painters. It becomes the almost universal habit of later artists to regard the flight as both sudden and secret, undertaken by Joseph and Mary, unattended, in the dawn of the morning, or "by night," so soon as Joseph had awaked from sleep. (Matthew 2:14.) Without a continuous miracle, which it is unnecessary in this case to suppose, such a lonely journey would have been nearly impracticable. Nor was instant flight necessary; for Herod's order for the massacre could not be issued until he had been convinced, by the protracted absence of the Wise Men, that he was "mocked of them."[1] In all probability the exact nature and extent of the danger was revealed to Joseph; and he would make the necessary preparations for his journey with such speed as he could, and depart "by night" indeed, but not in the instant of awakening from his dream. The ordinary impression seems to have been received from the words of the Gospel of Infancy: "Go into Egypt *as soon as the cock crows*."[2] And the interest of the flight is rendered more thrilling, in late compositions, by the introduction of armed pursuers. Giotto has given a far more quiet, deliberate, and probable character to the whole scene, while he has fully marked the fact of divine protection and command in the figure of the guiding angel. Nor is the picture less interesting in its marked expression of the night. The figures are all distinctly seen, and there is no broad distribution of the gloom; but the vigorous blackness of the dress of the attendant who holds the bridle, and the scattered glitter of the lights on the Madonna's robe, are enough to produce the required effect on the mind.

The figure of the Virgin is singularly dignified: the broad and severe curves traced by the hem and deepest folds of her dress materially conducing to the nobleness of the group. The Child is partly sustained by a band fastened round the Madonna's neck. The quaint and delicate pattern on this band, together with that of the embroidered edges of the dress, is of great value in opposing and making more manifest the severe and grave outlines of the whole figure, whose impressiveness is also partly increased by the rise of the mountain just above it, like a tent. A vulgar composer would have moved this peak to the right or left, and lost its power.

This mountain background is also of great use in deepening the sense of gloom and danger on the desert road. The trees represented as growing on the heights have probably been rendered indistinct by time. In early manuscripts such portions are invariably those which suffer most; the green (on which the leaves were once drawn with dark colours) mouldering away, and the lines of drawing with it. But even in what is here left there is noticeable more careful study of the distinction between the trees with thick spreading foliage, the group of two with light branches and few leaves, and the tree stripped and dead at the bottom of the ravine, than an historical painter would now think it consistent with his dignity to bestow.

1 [Ed. note, 1906: Matthew 2:16.]
2 [Ed. note, 1906: Infancy 4:3.]

XX
Massacre of the Innocents

Of all the series, this composition is the one which exhibits most of Giotto's weaknesses. All early work is apt to fail in the rendering of violent action: but Giotto is, in this instance, inferior not only to his successors, but to the feeblest of the miniature painters of the thirteenth century; while his imperfect drawing is seen at its worst in the nude figures of the children. It is, in fact, almost impossible to understand how any Italian, familiar with the eager gesticulations of the lower orders of his countrywomen on the smallest points of dispute with each other, should have been incapable of giving more adequate expression of true action and passion to the group of mothers; and, if I were not afraid of being accused of special pleading, I might insist at some length on a dim faith of my own that Giotto thought the actual agony and strivings of the probable scene unfit for pictorial treatment, or for common contemplation; and that he chose rather to give motionless types and personifications of the soldiers and women, than to use his strength and realistic faculty in bringing before the vulgar eye the unseemly struggle or unspeakable pain. The formal arrangement of the heap of corpses in the centre of the group; the crowded standing of the mothers, as in a choir of sorrow; the actual presence of Herod, to whom some of them appear to be appealing—all seem to me to mark this intention; and to make the composition only a symbol or shadow of the great deed of massacre, not a realization of its visible continuance at any moment. I will not press this conjecture; but will only add, that if it be so, I think Giotto was perfectly right; and that a picture thus conceived might have been deeply impressive, had it been more successfully executed; and a calmer, more continuous, comfortless grief expressed in the countenances of the women. Far better thus, than with the horrible analysis of agony, and detail of despair, with which this same scene, one which ought never to have been made the subject of painting at all, has been gloated over by artists of more degraded times.

XXI

The Young Christ in the Temple

This composition has suffered so grievously by time that even the portions of it which remain are seen to the greatest disadvantage. Little more than various conditions of scar and stain can be now traced, where were once the draperies of the figures in the shade, and the suspended garland and arches on the right hand of the spectator; and in endeavouring not to represent more than there is authority for, the draughtsman and engraver have necessarily produced a less satisfactory plate than most others of the series. But Giotto has also himself fallen considerably below his usual standard. The faces appear to be cold and hard; and the attitudes are as little graceful as expressive either of attention or surprise. The Madonna's action, stretching her arms to embrace her Son, is pretty; but, on the whole, the picture has no value; and this is the more remarkable, as there were fewer precedents of treatment in this case than in any of the others; and it might have been anticipated that Giotto would have put himself to some pains when the field of thought was comparatively new. The subject of Christ teaching in the Temple rarely occurs in manuscripts; but all the others were perpetually repeated in the service-books of the period.

XXII
The Baptism of Christ

This is a more interesting work than the last; but it is also gravely and strangely deficient in power of entering into the subject; and this, I think, is common with nearly all efforts that have hitherto been made at its representation. I have never seen a picture of the Baptism, by any painter whatever, which was not below the average power of the painter; and in this conception of Giotto's, the humility of St. John is entirely unexpressed, and the gesture of Christ has hardly any meaning: it neither is in harmony with the words, "Suffer it to be so now,"[1] which must have been uttered before the moment of actual baptism, nor does it in the slightest degree indicate the sense in the Redeemer of now entering upon the great work of His ministry. In the earlier representations of the subject, the humility of St. John is never lost sight of; there will be seen, for instance, an effort at expressing it by the slightly stooping attitude and bent knee, even in the very rude design given in outline on the following page. I have thought it worthwhile to set before the reader in this outline one example of the sort of traditional representations which were current throughout Christendom before Giotto arose. This instance is taken from a large choirbook, probably of French, certainly of Northern execution, towards the close of the thirteenth century;[2] and it is a very fair average example of the manner of design in the illuminated work of the period.

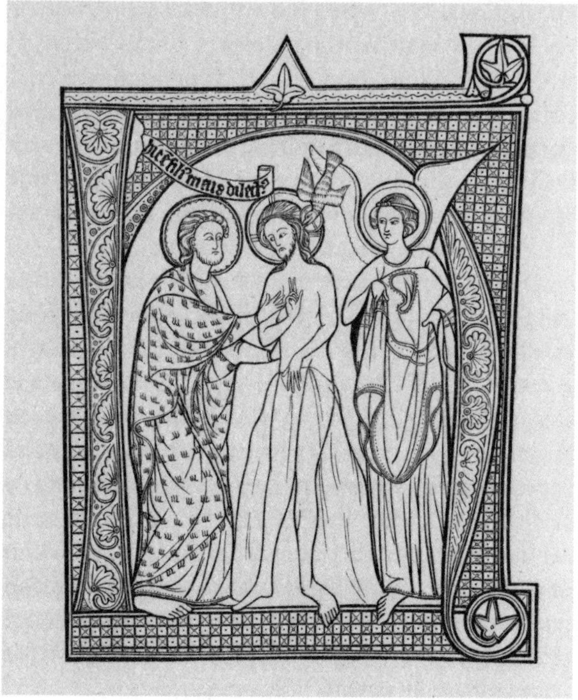

The Baptism of Christ, as depicted in a Medieval manuscript that belonged to John Ruskin.

The introduction of the scroll, with the legend, "This is My beloved Son," is both more true to the scriptural words, "Lo, a voice from heaven," and more reverent, than Giotto's introduction of the visible figure, as a type of the First Person of the Trinity.[3] The boldness with which this type is introduced increases precisely as the religious sentiment of art decreases; in the fifteenth century it becomes utterly revolting.

I have given this woodcut for another reason also: to explain more clearly the mode in which Giotto deduced the strange form which he has given to the stream of the Jordan. In the earlier Northern works it is merely a green wave, rising to the Saviour's waist, as seen in the woodcut. Giotto, for the sake of getting standing ground for his figures, gives *shores* to this wave, retaining its swelling form in the centre—a very painful and unsuccessful attempt at reconciling typical drawing with laws of perspective. Or perhaps it is less to be regarded as an effort at progress, than as an awkward combination of the Eastern and Western types of the Jordan. In the difference between these types there is matter of some interest. Lord Lindsay, who merely characterizes this work of Giotto's as "the Byzantine composition,"[4] thus describes the usual Byzantine manner of representing the Baptism:

"The Saviour stands immersed to the middle in Jordan, *flowing between two deep and rocky banks*, on one of which stands St. John, pouring the water on His head, and on the other two angels hold His robes. The Holy

Spirit descends upon Him as a dove, in a stream of light, from God the Father, usually represented by a hand from Heaven. Two of John's disciples stand behind him as spectators. Frequently *the river god of Jordan* reclines with his oars in the corner.... In the Baptistery at Ravenna, the robe is supported, not by an angel, but by the river deity *Jordann* (Iordanes?), who holds in his left hand a reed as his sceptre."[5]

Now in this mode of representing rivers there is something more than the mere Pagan tradition lingering through the wrecks of the Eastern Empire. A river, in the East and South, is necessarily recognized more distinctly as a beneficent power than in the West and North. The narrowest and feeblest stream is felt to have an influence on the life of mankind; and is counted among the possessions, or honoured among the deities, of the people who dwell beside it. Hence the importance given, in the Byzantine compositions, to the name and speciality of the Jordan stream. In the North such peculiar definiteness and importance can never be attached to the name of any single fountain. Water, in its various forms of streamlet, rain, or river, is felt as a universal gift of Heaven, not as an inheritance of a particular spot of earth. Hence, with the Gothic artists generally, the personality of the Jordan is lost in the green and nameless wave; and the simple rite of the Baptism is dwelt upon, without endeavouring, as Giotto has done, to draw the attention to the rocky shores of Bethabara and Aenon, or to the fact that "there was much water there."[6]

1 [Ed. note, 1906: Matthew 3:15.]

2 The exact date, 1290, is given in the title page of the volume.

3 [Ed. note, 1906: Matthew 3:17.]

4 [Ed. note, 1906: Lindsay, *Christian Art*, vol. 2, p. 189.]

5 [Ed. note, 1906: Lindsay, *Christian Art*, vol. 1, pp. 88, 89. The italics and the insertion "(Iordanes?)" are Ruskin's.]

6 [Ed. note, 1906: "These things were done in Bethabara beyond Jordan" (John 1:28). "And John was also baptizing in Aenon, near to Salim, because there was much water there" (John 3:23).]

XXIII
The Marriage in Cana

It is strange that the sweet significance of this first of the miracles should have been lost sight of by nearly all artists after Giotto; and that no effort was made by them to conceive the circumstances of it in simplicity. The poverty of the family in which the marriage took place—proved sufficiently by the fact that a carpenter's wife not only was asked as a chief guest, but even had authority over the servants—is shown further to have been distressful, or at least embarrassed, poverty by their want of wine on such an occasion. It was not certainly to remedy an accident of careless provision, but to supply a need sorrowfully betraying the narrow circumstances of His hosts, that our Lord wrought the beginning of miracles.[1] Many mystic meanings have been sought in the act, which, though there is no need to deny, there is little evidence to certify: but we may joyfully accept, as its first indisputable meaning, that of simple kindness; the wine being provided here, when needed, as the bread and fish were afterwards for the hungry multitudes. The whole value of the miracle, in its serviceable tenderness, is at once effaced when the marriage is supposed, as by Veronese and other artists of later times, to have taken place at the house of a rich man. For the rest, Giotto sufficiently implies, by the lifted hand of the Madonna, and the action of the fingers of the bridegroom, as if they held sacramental bread, that there lay a deeper meaning under the miracle for those who could accept it. How all miracle *is* accepted by common humanity, he has also shown in the figure of the ruler of the feast, drinking. This unregarding forgetfulness of present spiritual power is similarly marked by Veronese, by placing the figure of a fool with his bauble immediately underneath that of Christ, and by making a cat play with her shadow in one of the wine vases.

It is to be remembered, however, in examining all pictures of this subject, that the miracle was not made manifest to all the guests—to none indeed, seemingly, except Christ's own disciples: the ruler of the feast, and probably most of those present (except the servants who drew the water), knew or observed nothing of what was passing, and merely thought the good wine had been "kept until now."[2]

1 [Ed. note, 1906: John 2:11.]

2 [Ed. note, 1906: John 2:9–10.]

XXIV
The Raising of Lazarus

In consequence of the intermediate position which Giotto occupies between the Byzantine and Naturalist schools, two relations of treatment are to be generally noted in his work. As compared with the Byzantines, he is a realist, whose power consists in the introduction of living character and various incidents, modifying the formerly received Byzantine symbols. So far as he has to do this, he is a realist of the purest kind, endeavouring always to conceive events precisely as they were likely to have happened; not to idealize them into forms artfully impressive to the spectator. But insofar as he was compelled to retain, or did not wish to reject, the figurative character of the Byzantine symbols, he stands opposed to succeeding realists, in the quantity of meaning which probably lies hidden in any composition, as well as in the simplicity with which he will probably treat it, in order to enforce or guide to this meaning: the figures being often letters of a hieroglyphic, which he will not multiply, lest he should lose in force of suggestion what he gained in dramatic interest.

None of the compositions display more clearly this typical and reflective character than that of the Raising of Lazarus. Later designers dwell on vulgar conditions of wonder or horror, such as they could conceive likely to attend the resuscitation of a corpse; but with Giotto the physical reanimation is the type of a spiritual one, and, though shown to be miraculous, is yet in all its deeper aspects unperturbed, and calm in awfulness. It is also visibly gradual. "His face was bound about with a napkin."[1] The nearest Apostle has withdrawn the covering from the face, and looks for the command which shall restore it from wasted corruption, and sealed blindness, to living power and light.

Nor is it, I believe, without meaning, that the two Apostles, if indeed they are intended for Apostles, who stand at Lazarus's side, wear a different dress from those who follow Christ. I suppose them to be intended for images of the Christian and Jewish Churches in their ministration to the dead soul: the one removing its bonds, but looking to Christ for the word and power of life; the other inactive and helpless—the veil upon its face—in dread; while the principal figure fulfils the order it receives in fearless simplicity.

1 [Ed. note, 1906: John 11:44.]

XXV
The Entry into Jerusalem

This design suffers much from loss of colour in translation. Its decorative effect depends on the deep blue ground, relieving the delicate foliage and the local colours of dresses and architecture. It is also one of those which are most directly opposed to modern feeling: the sympathy of the spectator with the passion of the crowd being somewhat rudely checked by the grotesque action of two of the foremost figures. We ought, however, rather to envy the deep seriousness which could not be moved from dwelling on the real power of the scene by any ungracefulness or familiarity of circumstance. Among men whose minds are rightly toned, nothing is ludicrous: it must, if an act, be either right or wrong, noble or base; if a thing seen, it must either be ugly or beautiful: and what is either wrong or deformed is not, among noble persons, in anywise subject for laughter; but, in the precise degree of its wrongness or deformity, a subject of horror. All perception of what, in the modern European mind, falls under the general head of the ludicrous, is either childish or profane; often healthy, as indicative of vigorous animal life, but always degraded in its relation to manly conditions of thought. It has a secondary use in its power of detecting vulgar imposture; but it only obtains this power by denying the highest truths.

XXVI

The Expulsion from the Temple

More properly, the Expulsion from the outer Court of the Temple (Court of Gentiles), as Giotto has indicated by placing the porch of the Temple itself in the background.

The design shows, as clearly as that of the Massacre of the Innocents, Giotto's want of power, and partly of desire, to represent rapid or forceful action. The raising of the right hand, not holding any scourge,[1] resembles the action afterwards adopted by Orcagna, and finally by Michelangelo in his Last Judgment: and my belief is that Giotto considered this act of Christ's as partly typical of the final judgment, the Pharisees being placed on the left hand, and the disciples on the right. From the faded remains of the fresco, the draughtsman could not determine what animals are intended by those on the left hand. But the most curious incident (so far as I know, found only in this design of the Expulsion, no subsequent painter repeating it) is the sheltering of the two children, one of them carrying a dove, under the arm and cloak of two disciples. Many meanings might easily be suggested in this; but I see no evidence for the adoption of any distinct one.

1 [Ed. note, 1900: In the Arundel Society's woodcut there was no scourge, and Ruskin wrote evidently with the woodcut and not the original before him. The scourge is, however, plainly visible in the original, and its omission was the draughtsman's error.]

XXVII
The Hiring of Judas

The only point of material interest presented by this design is the decrepit and distorted shadow of the demon, respecting which it may be well to remind the reader that all the great Italian thinkers concurred in assuming decrepitude or disease, as well as ugliness, to be a characteristic of all natures of evil. Whatever the extent of the power granted to evil spirits, it was always abominable and contemptible; no element of beauty or heroism was ever allowed to remain, however obscured, in the aspect of a fallen angel. Also, the demoniacal nature was shown in acts of betrayal, torture, or wanton hostility; never in valiancy or perseverance of contest. I recollect no medieval demon who shows as much insulting, resisting, or contending power as Bunyan's Apollyon. They can only cheat, undermine, and mock; never overthrow. Judas, as we should naturally anticipate, has not in this scene the nimbus of an Apostle; yet we shall find it restored to him in the next design. We shall discover the reason of this only by a careful consideration of the meaning of that fresco.

XXVIII
The Last Supper

I have not examined the original fresco with care enough to be able to say whether the uninteresting quietness of its design is redeemed by more than ordinary attention to expression; it is one of the least attractive subjects in the Arena Chapel, and always sure to be passed over in any general observation of the series: nevertheless, however unfavourably it may at first contrast with the designs of later masters, and especially with Leonardo's, the reader should not fail to observe that Giotto's aim, had it been successful, was the higher of the two, as giving truer rendering of the probable fact. There is no distinct evidence, in the sacred text, of the annunciation of coming treachery having produced among the disciples the violent surprise and agitation represented by Leonardo. Naturally, they would not at first understand what was meant. They knew nothing distinctly of the machinations of the priests; and so little of the character or purposes of Judas, that even after he had received the sop which was to point him out to the others as false—and after they had heard the injunction, "That thou doest, do quickly"—the other disciples had still no conception of the significance, either of the saying, or the act: they thought that Christ meant he was to buy something for the feast. Nay, Judas himself, so far from starting, as a convicted traitor, and thereby betraying himself, as in Leonardo's picture, had not, when Christ's first words were uttered, any immediately active intention formed. The devil had not entered into him until he received the sop.

The passage in St. John's account[1] is a curious one, and little noticed; but it marks very distinctly the paralysed state of the man's mind. He had talked with the priests, covenanted with them, and even sought opportunity[2] to bring Jesus into their hands; but while such opportunity was wanting, the act had never presented itself fully to him for adoption or rejection. He had toyed with it, dreamed over it, hesitated, and procrastinated over it, as a stupid and cowardly person would, such as traitors are apt to be. But the way of retreat was yet open; the conquest of the tempter not complete. Only after receiving the sop the idea *finally* presented itself clearly, and was accepted, "Tonight, while He is in the garden, I can do it; and I will." And Giotto has indicated this distinctly by giving Judas still the Apostle's nimbus, both in this subject and in that of the Washing of the Feet; while it is taken away in the previous subject of the Hiring, and the following one of the Seizure: thus it fluctuates, expires, and reillumines itself, until his fall is consummated. This being the general state of the Apostles' knowledge, the words "One of you shall betray Me"[3] would excite no feeling in their minds correspondent to that with which we now read the prophetic sentence. What this "giving up" of their Master meant became a question of bitter and self-searching thought with them—gradually of intense sorrow and questioning. But had they understood it in the sense we now understand it, they would never have each asked, "Lord, is it I?" Peter believed himself incapable even of *denying* Christ:[4] and of giving Him up to death for money, every one of His true disciples *knew* themselves incapable; the thought never occurred to them. In slowly increasing wonder and sorrow (*ἤϱξαντο λυπεῖσθαι*, Mark 14:19), not knowing what was meant, they asked one by one, with pauses between, "Is it I?" and another, "Is it I?" and this so quietly and timidly that the one who was lying on Christ's breast never stirred from his place; and Peter, afraid to speak, signed to him to ask who it was. One further circumstance, showing that this was the real state of their minds, we shall find Giotto take cognizance of in the next fresco.

1 [Ed. note, 1906: John 13:26 et seq.]
2 [Ed. note, 1906: Matthew 26:16.]
3 [Ed. note, 1906: Matthew 26:21, 22.]
4 [Ed. note, 1906: Matthew 26:35.]

XXIX
The Washing of the Feet

In this design, it will be observed, there are still the twelve disciples, and the nimbus is yet given to Judas (though, as it were, setting, his face not being seen).[1]

Considering the deep interest and importance of every circumstance of the Last Supper, I cannot understand how preachers and commentators pass by the difficulty of clearly understanding the periods indicated in St. John's account of it. It seems that Christ must have risen while they were still eating, must have washed their feet as they sat or reclined at the table, just as the Magdalen had washed His own feet in the Pharisee's house; that, this done, He returned to the table, and the disciples continuing to eat, presently gave the sop to Judas. For St. John says that he, having received the sop, went *immediately* out; yet that Christ had washed his feet is certain, from the words, "Ye are clean, but not all."[2] Whatever view the reader may, on deliberation, choose to accept, Giotto's is clear, namely, that though not cleansed by the baptism, Judas was yet capable of being cleansed. The devil had not entered into him at the time of the washing of the feet, and he retains the sign of an Apostle.

The composition is one of the most beautiful of the series, especially owing to the submissive grace of the two standing figures.

1 [Ed. note, 1900: There is, I think, some error here, owing to the loss of likeness in the faces in the reproduction of the Arundel Society. Judas is not hidden behind the figure to the extreme right, but is the centre of the three figures to the extreme left. This is clear from the face, the likeness of which is carefully preserved in this and the two preceding designs.]

2 [Ed. note, 1906: John 13:30, 10.]

XXX
The Kiss of Judas

For the first time we have Giotto's idea of the face of the traitor clearly shown. It is not, I think, traceable through any of the previous series; and it has often surprised me to observe how impossible it was in the works of almost any of the sacred painters to determine by the mere cast of feature which was meant for the false Apostle. Here, however, Giotto's theory of physiognomy, and together with it his idea of the character of Judas, are perceivable enough. It is evident that he looks upon Judas mainly as a sensual dullard, and foul-brained fool; a man in no respect exalted in bad eminence of treachery above the mass of common traitors, but merely a distinct type of the eternal treachery to good, in vulgar men, which stoops beneath, and opposes in its appointed measure, the life and efforts of all noble persons, their natural enemies in this world; as the slime lies under a clear stream running through an earthy meadow. Our careless and thoughtless English use of the word into which the Greek "Diabolos" has been shortened, blinds us in general to the meaning of "Devilry," which, in its essence, is nothing else than slander, or traitorhood—the accusing and giving up of good. In particular it has blinded us to the meaning of Christ's words, "Have not I chosen you twelve, and one of you is a traitor and accuser?" and led us to think that the "one of you is a devil"[1] indicated some greater than human wickedness in Judas; whereas the practical meaning of the entire fact of Judas's ministry and fall is that out of any twelve men chosen for the forwarding of any purpose—or, much more, out of any twelve men we meet—one, probably, is or will be a Judas.

The modern German renderings of all the scenes of Christ's life in which the traitor is conspicuous are very curious in their vulgar misunderstanding of the history, and their consequent endeavours to represent Judas as more diabolic than selfish, treacherous, and stupid men are in all their generations. They paint him usually projected against strong effects of light, in lurid chiaroscuro—enlarging the whites of his eyes, and making him frown, grin, and gnash his teeth on all occasions, so as to appear among the other Apostles invariably in the aspect of a Gorgon.

How much more deeply Giotto has fathomed the fact, I believe all men will admit who have sufficient purity and abhorrence of falsehood to recognize it in its daily presence, and who know how the devil's strongest work is done for him by men who are too bestial to understand what they betray.

1 [Ed. note, 1906: John 6:70.]

XXXI
Christ Before Caiaphas

Little is to be observed in this design of any distinctive merit; it is only a somewhat completer version of the ordinary representation given in illuminated missals and other conventual work, suggesting, as if they had happened at the same moment, the answer, "If I have spoken evil, bear witness of the evil,"[1] and the accusation of blasphemy which causes the high priest to rend his clothes.

Apparently distrustful of his power of obtaining interest of a higher kind, Giotto has treated the enrichments more carefully than usual, down even to the steps of the high priest's seat. The torch and barred shutters conspicuously indicate its being now dead of night. That the torch is darker than the chamber, if not an error in the drawing, is probably the consequence of a darkening alteration in the yellow colours used for the flame.

1 [Ed. note, 1906: John 18:23.]

XXXII
The Scourging of Christ

It is characteristic of Giotto's rational and human view of all subjects admitting such aspect that he has insisted here chiefly on the dejection and humiliation of Christ, making no attempt to suggest to the spectator any other divinity than that of patience made perfect through suffering.[1] Angelico's conception of the same subject is higher and more mystical. He takes the moment when Christ is blindfolded, and exaggerates almost into monstrosity the vileness of feature and bitterness of sneer in the questioners, "Prophesy unto us, who is he that smote thee";[2] but the bearing of the person of Christ is entirely calm and unmoved; and His eyes, open, are seen through the blinding veil, indicating the ceaseless omniscience.

This mystical rendering is, again, rejected by the later realistic painters; but while the earlier designers, with Giotto at their head, dwelt chiefly on the humiliation and the mockery, later painters dwelt on the physical pain. In Titian's great picture of this subject in the Louvre, one of the executioners is thrusting the thorn crown down upon the brow with his rod, and the action of Christ is that of a person suffering extreme physical agony.

No representations of the scene exist, to my knowledge, in which the mockery is either sustained with indifference, or rebuked by any stern or appealing expression of feature; yet one of these two forms of endurance would appear, to a modern habit of thought, the most natural and probable.

1 [Ed. note, 1906: Hebrews 2:10.]
2 [Ed. note, 1906: Matthew 26:68.]

XXXIII
Christ Bearing His Cross

This design is one of great nobleness and solemnity in the isolation of the principal figure, and removal of all motives of interest depending on accessories, or merely temporary incidents. Even the Virgin and her attendant women are kept in the background; all appeal for sympathy through physical suffering is disdained. Christ is not represented as borne down by the weight of the Cross, nor as urged forward by the impatience of the executioners. The thing to be shown—the unspeakable mystery—is the simple fact, the Bearing of the Cross by the Redeemer. It would be vain to compare the respective merits or value of a design thus treated, and of one like Veronese's of this same subject, in which every essential accessory and probable incident is completely conceived. The abstract and symbolical suggestion will always appeal to one order of minds, the dramatic completeness to another. Unquestionably, the last is the greater achievement of intellect, but the manner and habit of thought are perhaps loftier in Giotto. Veronese leads us to perceive the reality of the act, and Giotto to understand its intention.

XXXIV
The Crucifixion

The treatment of this subject was, in Giotto's time, so rigidly fixed by tradition that it was out of his power to display any of his own special modes of thought; and, as in the Bearing of the Cross, so here, but yet more distinctly, the temporary circumstances are little regarded, the significance of the event being alone cared for. But even long after this time, in all the pictures of the Crucifixion by the great masters, with the single exception perhaps of that by Tintoretto in the Church of San Cassiano at Venice, there is a tendency to treat the painting as a symmetrical image, or collective symbol of sacred mysteries, rather than as a dramatic representation. Even in Tintoretto's great Crucifixion in the School of San Rocco, the group of fainting women forms a kind of pedestal for the Cross. The flying angels in the composition before us are thus also treated with a restraint hardly passing the limits of decorative symbolism. The fading away of their figures into flame-like cloud may perhaps be founded on the verse, "He maketh His angels spirits; His ministers a flame of fire" (though erroneously, the right reading of that verse being, "He maketh the winds His messengers, and the flaming fire His servant");[1] but it seems to me to give a greater sense of possible truth than the entire figures, treading the clouds with naked feet, of Perugino and his successors.

1 [Ed. note, 1906: Psalms 104:4 (quoted in Hebrews 1:7).]

XXXV
The Entombment

I do not consider that in fulfilling the task of interpreter entrusted to me, with respect to this series of engravings, I may in general permit myself to unite with it the duty of a critic. But in the execution of a laborious series of engravings, some must of course be better, some worse; and it would be unjust, no less to the reader than to Giotto, if I allowed this plate to pass without some admission of its inadequacy. It may possibly have been treated with a little less care than the rest, in the knowledge that the finished plate, already in the possession of the members of the Arundel Society, superseded any effort with inferior means; be that as it may, the tenderness of Giotto's composition is, in the engraving before us, lost to an unusual degree.

It may be generally observed that the passionateness of the sorrow both of the Virgin and disciples, is represented by Giotto and all great following designers as reaching its crisis at the Entombment, not at the Crucifixion. The expectation that, after experiencing every form of human suffering, Christ would yet come down from the cross, or in some other visible and immediate manner achieve for Himself the victory, might be conceived to have supported in a measure the minds of those among His disciples who watched by His cross. But when the agony was closed by actual death, and the full strain was put upon their faith, by their laying in the sepulchre, wrapped in His grave clothes, Him in whom they trusted "that it had been He which should have redeemed Israel,"[1] their sorrow became suddenly hopeless; a gulf of horror opened, almost at unawares, under their feet; and in the poignancy of her astonied despair, it was no marvel that the agony of the Madonna in the Pietà became subordinately associated in the mind of the early Church with that of their Lord Himself—a type of consummate human suffering.

1 [Ed. note, 1906: Luke 24:21.]

XXXVI
The Resurrection

Quite one of the loveliest designs of the series. It was a favourite subject with Giotto; meeting, in all its conditions, his love of what was most mysterious, yet most comforting and full of hope, in the doctrines of his religion. His joy in the fact of the Resurrection, his sense of its function, as the key and primal truth of Christianity, was far too deep to allow him to dwell on any of its minor circumstances, as later designers did, representing the moment of bursting the tomb, and the supposed terror of its guards. With Giotto the leading thought is not of physical reanimation, nor of the momentarily exerted power of breaking the bars of the grave; but the consummation of Christ's work in the first manifesting to human eyes, and the eyes of one who had loved Him and believed in Him, His power to take again the life He had laid down. This first appearance to her out of whom He had cast seven devils[1] is indeed the very central fact of the Resurrection. The keepers had not seen Christ; they had seen only the angel descending, whose countenance was like lightning: for fear of him they became as dead; yet this fear, though great enough to cause them to swoon, was so far conquered at the return of morning that they were ready to take money payment for giving a false report of the circumstances.[2] The Magdalen, therefore, is the first witness of the Resurrection; to the love, for whose sake much had been forgiven,[3] this gift is also first given; and as the first witness of the truth, so she is the first messenger of the Gospel. To the Apostles it was granted to proclaim the Resurrection to all nations; but the Magdalen was bidden to proclaim it to the Apostles.[4]

In the chapel of the Bargello, Giotto has rendered this scene with yet more passionate sympathy. Here, however, its significance is more thoughtfully indicated through all the accessories, down even to the withered trees above the sepulchre, while those of the garden burst into leaf. This could hardly escape notice, when the barren boughs were compared by the spectator with the rich foliage of the neighbouring designs, though, in the detached plate, it might easily be lost sight of.

1 [Ed. note, 1906: Mark 16:9.]
2 [Ed. note, 1906: Matthew 28:2–4, 12–15.]
3 [Ed. note, 1906: Luke 7:47.]
4 [Ed. note, 1906: Matthew 28:10, 19.]

XXXVII
The Ascension

Giotto continues to exert all his strength on these closing subjects. None of the Byzantine or earlier Italian painters ventured to introduce the entire figure of Christ in this scene: they showed the feet only, concealing the body; according to the text, "a cloud received Him out of their sight."[1] This composition, graceful as it is daring, conveys the idea of ascending motion more forcibly than any that I remember by other than Venetian painters. Much of its power depends on the continuity of line obtained by the half-floating figures of the two warning angels.

I cannot understand why this subject was so seldom treated by religious painters: for the harmony of Christian creed depends as much upon it as on the Resurrection itself; while the circumstances of the Ascension, in their brightness, promise, miraculousness, and direct appeal to all the assembled Apostles, seem more fitted to attract the joyful contemplation of all who received the faith. How morbid, and how deeply to be mourned, was the temper of the Church which could not be satisfied without perpetual representation of the tortures of Christ; but rarely dwelt on His triumph! How more than strange the concessions to this feebleness by its greatest teachers; such as that of Titian, who, though he paints the Assumption of the Madonna rather than a Pietà, paints the Scourging and the Entombment of Christ, with his best power—but never the Ascension!

1 [Ed. note, 1906: Acts 1:9.]

XXXVIII
The Descent of the Holy Spirit

This last subject of the series, the quietest and least interesting in treatment, yet illustrates sadly, and forcibly, the vital difference between ancient and modern art.

The worst characters of modern work result from its constant appeal to our desire of change, and pathetic excitement; while the best features of the elder art appealed to love of contemplation. It would appear to be the object of the truest artists to give permanence to images such as we should always desire to behold, and might behold without agitation; while the inferior branches of design are concerned with the acuter passions which depend on the turn of a narrative, or the course of an emotion. Where it is possible to unite these two sources of pleasure, and, as in the Assumption of Titian, an action of absorbing interest is united with perfect and perpetual elements of beauty, the highest point of conception would appear to have been touched: but in the degree in which the interest of action *supersedes* beauty of form and colour, the art is lowered; and where real deformity enters, in any other degree than as a momentary shadow or opposing force, the art is illegitimate. Such art can exist only by accident, when a nation has forgotten or betrayed the eternal purposes of its genius, and gives birth to painters whom it cannot teach, and to teachers whom it will not hear. The best talents of all our English painters have been spent either in endeavours to find room for the expression of feelings which no master guided to a worthy end, or to obtain the attention of a public whose mind was dead to natural beauty, by sharpness of satire, or variety of dramatic circumstance.

The work to which England is now devoting herself withdraws her eyes from beauty, as her heart from rest; nor do I conceive any revival of great art to be possible among us while the nation continues in its present temper. As long as it can bear to see misery and squalor in its streets, it can neither invent nor accept human beauty in its pictures; and so long as in passion of rivalry, or thrift of gain, it crushes the roots of happiness, and forsakes the ways of peace, the great souls whom it may chance to produce will all pass away from it helpless, in error, in wrath, or in silence. Amiable visionaries may retire into the delight of devotional abstraction, strong men of the world may yet hope to do service by their rebuke or their satire; but for the clear sight of Love there will be no horizon, for its quiet words no answer; nor any place for the art which alone is faithfully Religious, because it is Lovely and True.

Plates

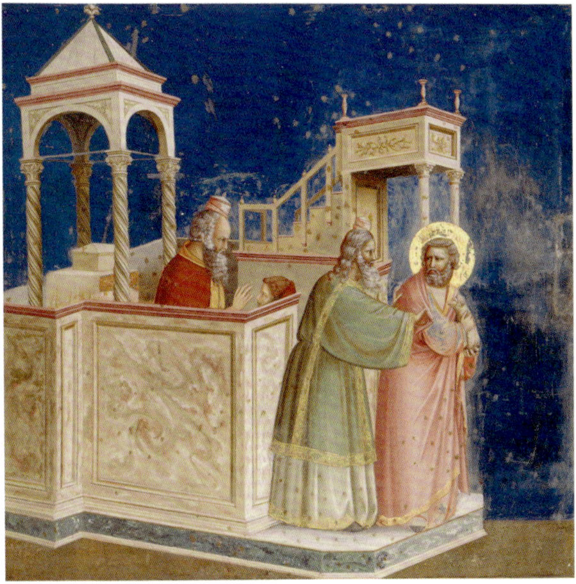

I

The Rejection of Joachim's Offering

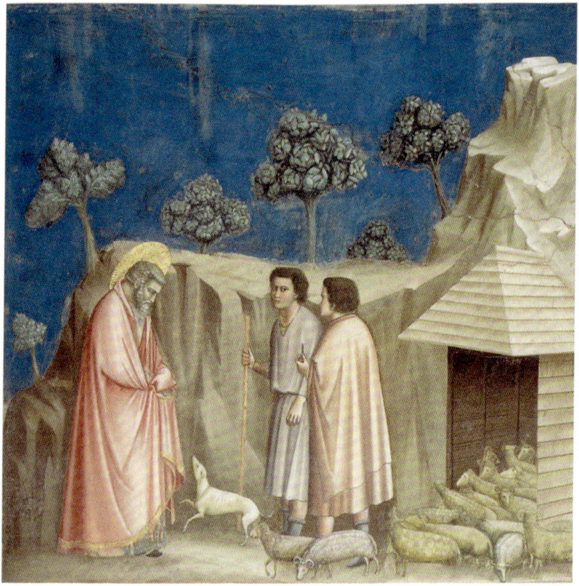

11
Joachim Retires to the Sheepfold

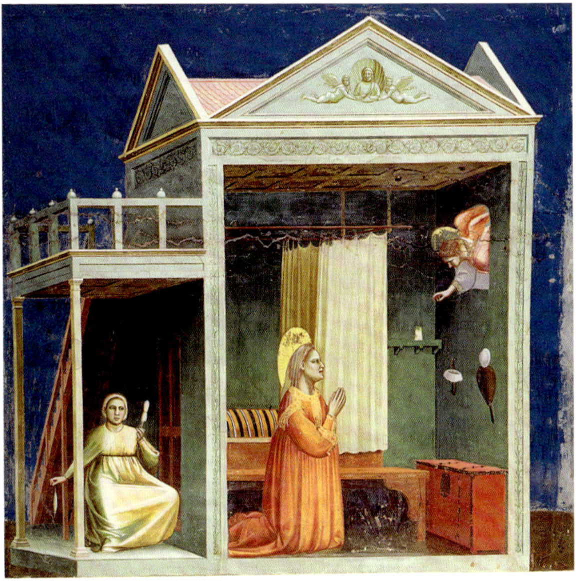

III

The Angel Appears to Anna

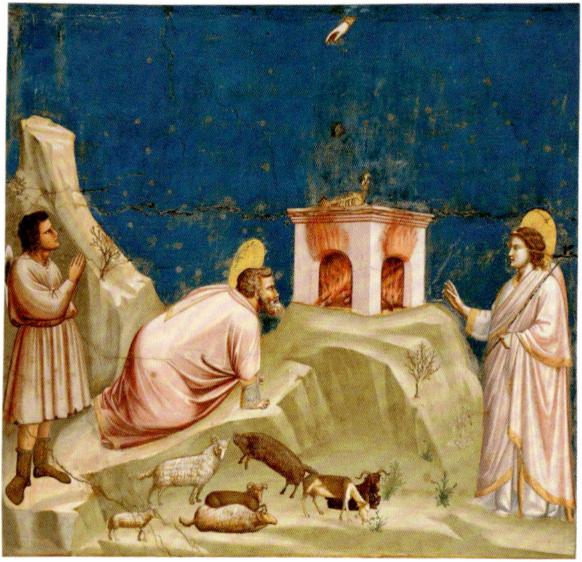

IV

The Sacrifice of Joachim

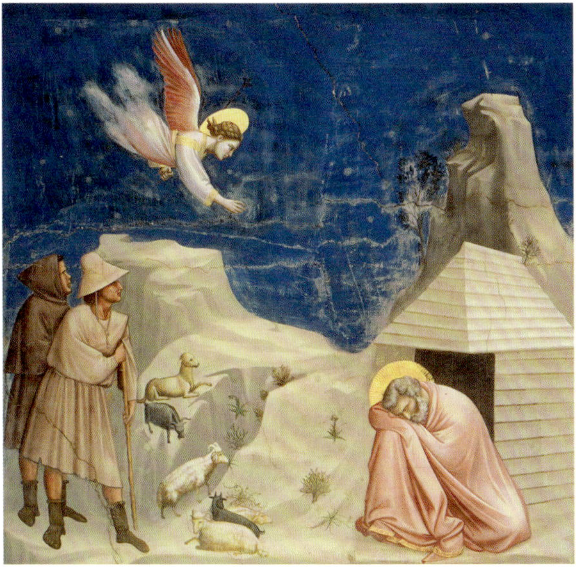

V

The Angel (Raphael) Appears to Joachim

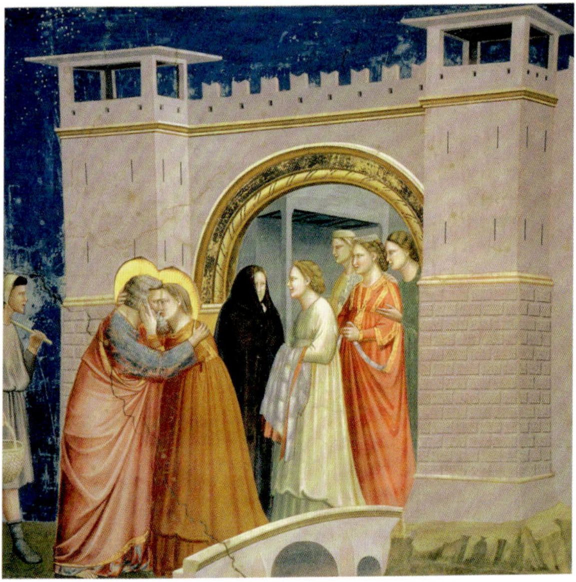

VI

The Meeting at the Golden Gate

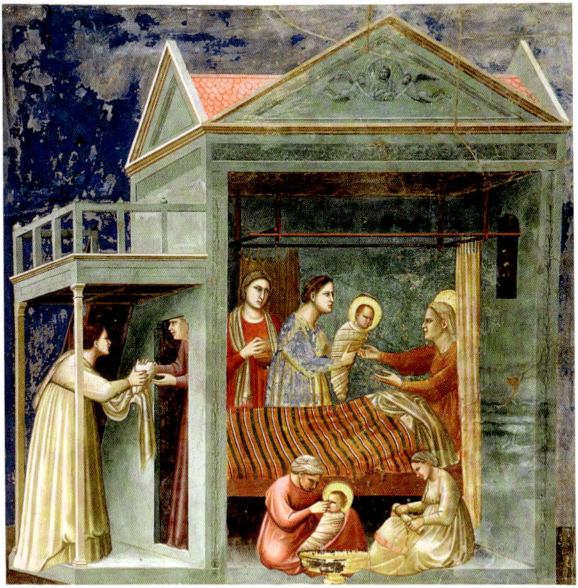

VII

The Birth of the Virgin

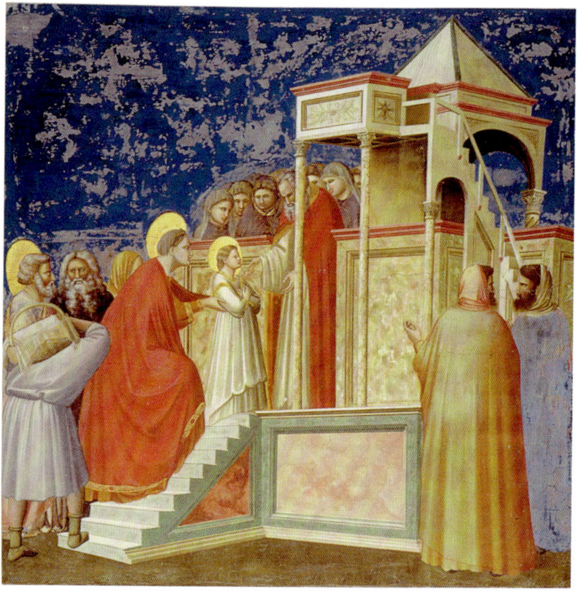

VIII

The Presentation of the Virgin

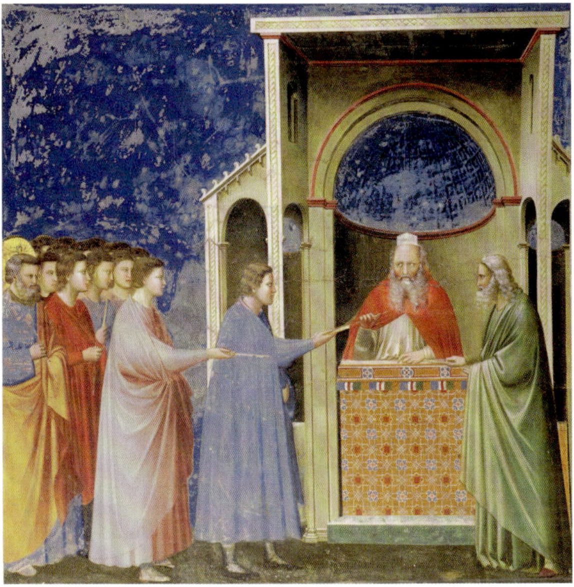

IX

The Rods Are Brought to the High Priest

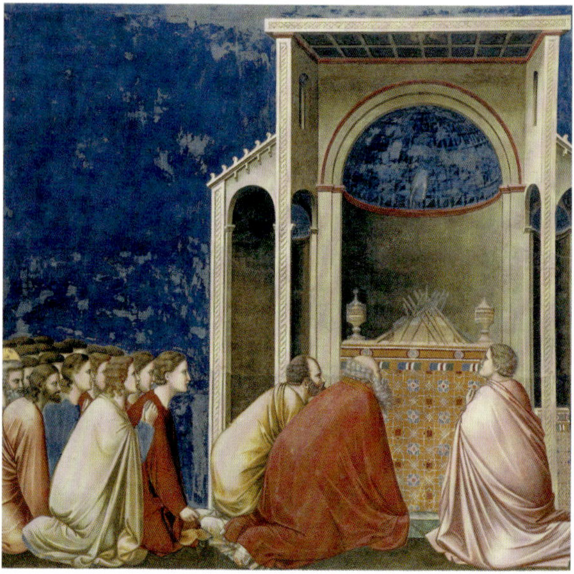

X

The Watching of the Rods at the Altar

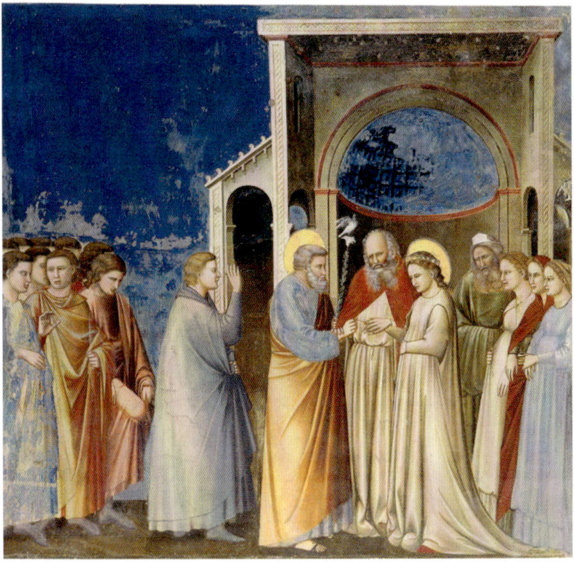

XI
The Betrothal of the Virgin

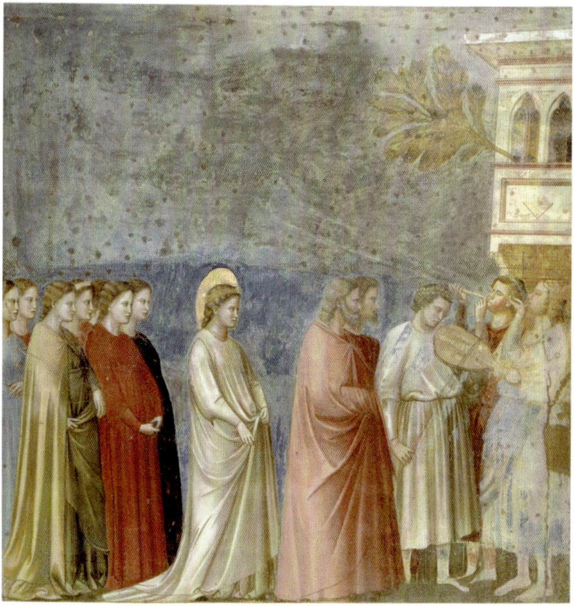

XII

The Virgin Mary Returns to Her House

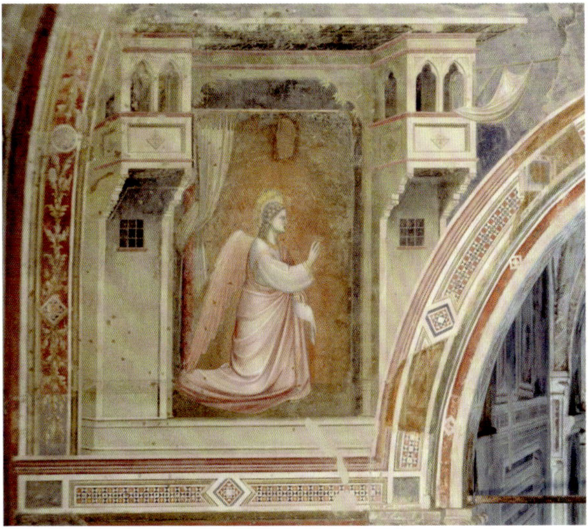

XIII
The Annunciation—The Angel Gabriel

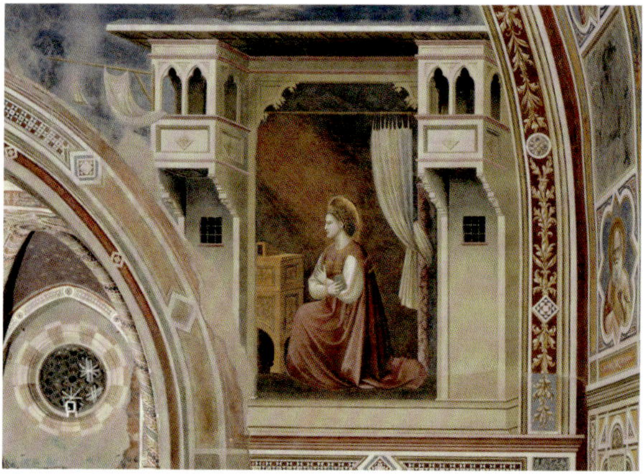

XIV

The Annunciation—The Virgin Mary

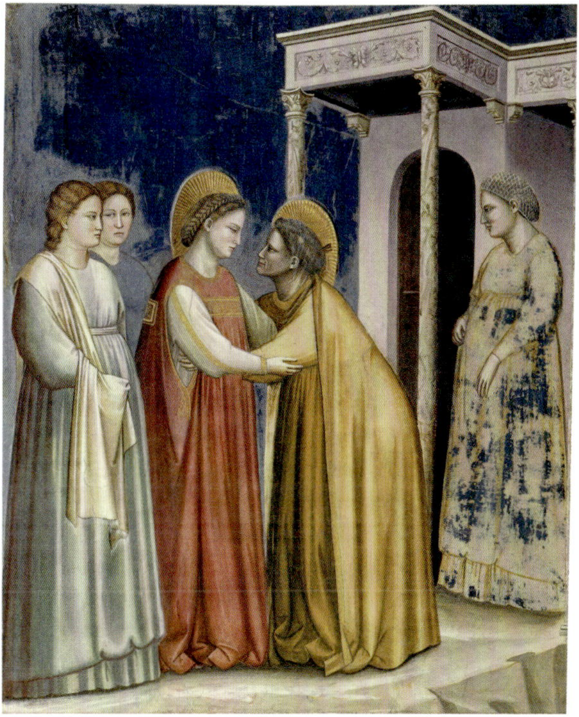

XV
The Salutation

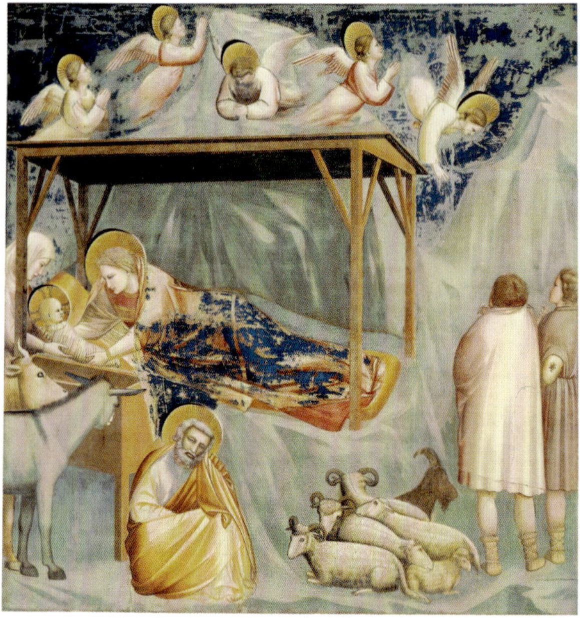

XVI
The Nativity

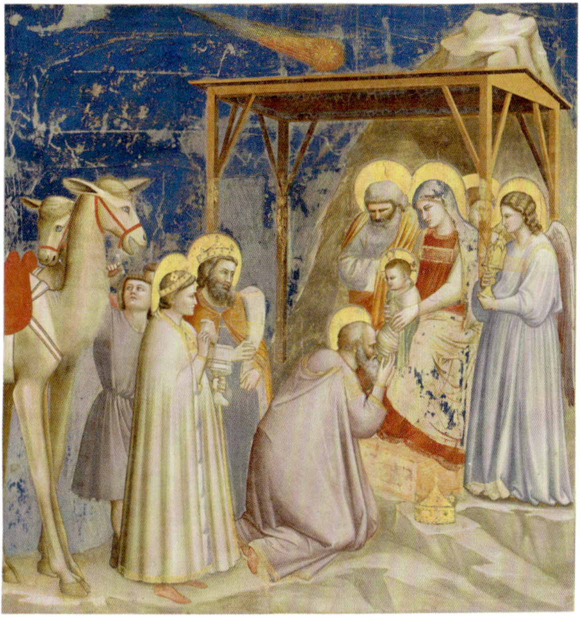

XVII

The Wise Men's Offering

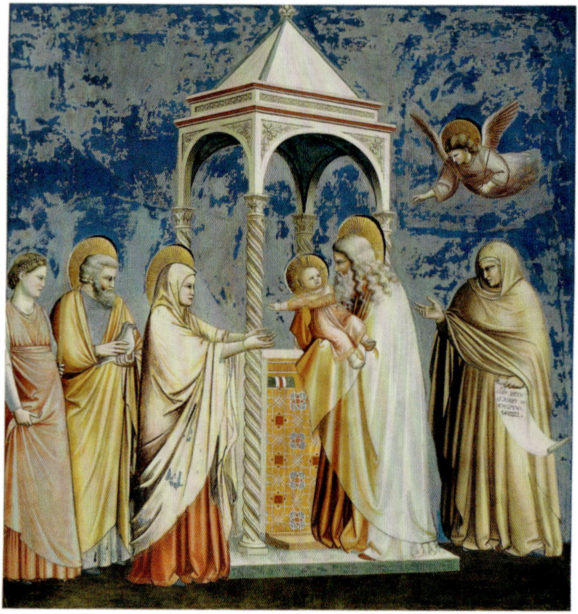

XVIII

The Presentation in the Temple

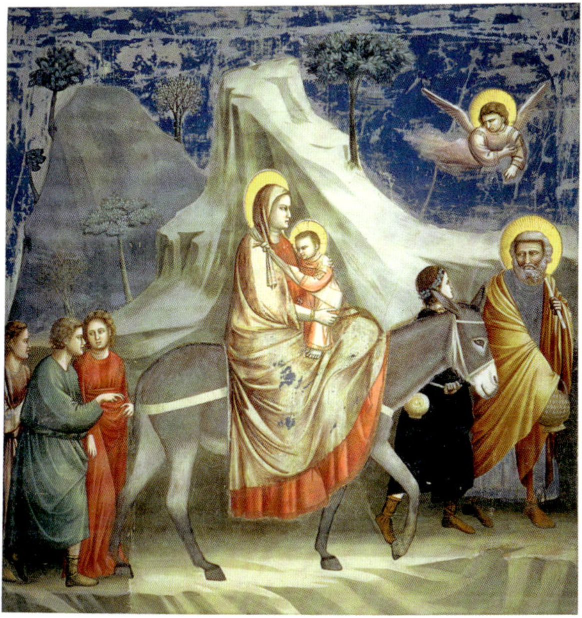

XIX
The Flight into Egypt

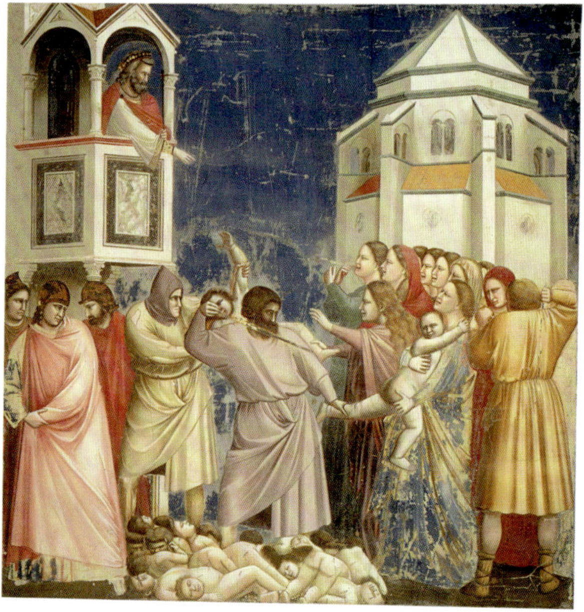

XX

Massacre of the Innocents

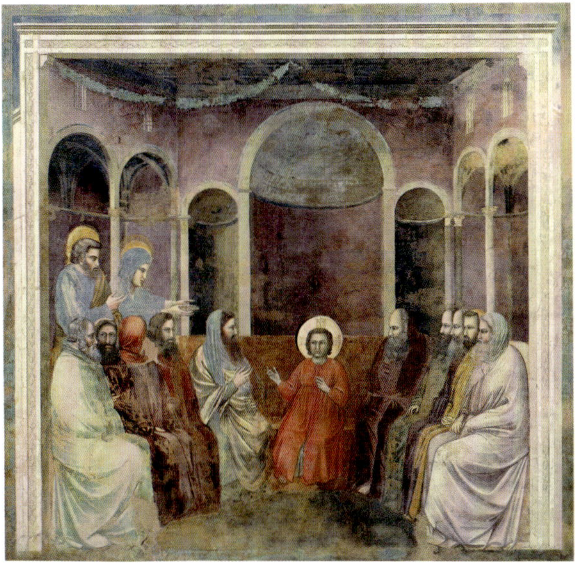

XXI
The Young Christ in the Temple

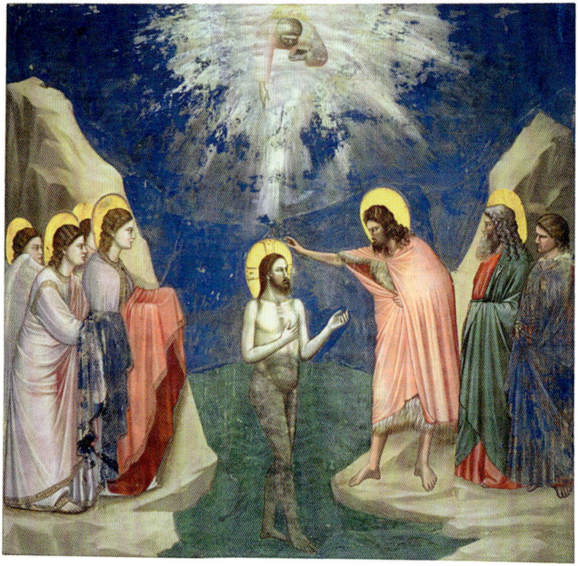

XXII

The Baptism of Christ

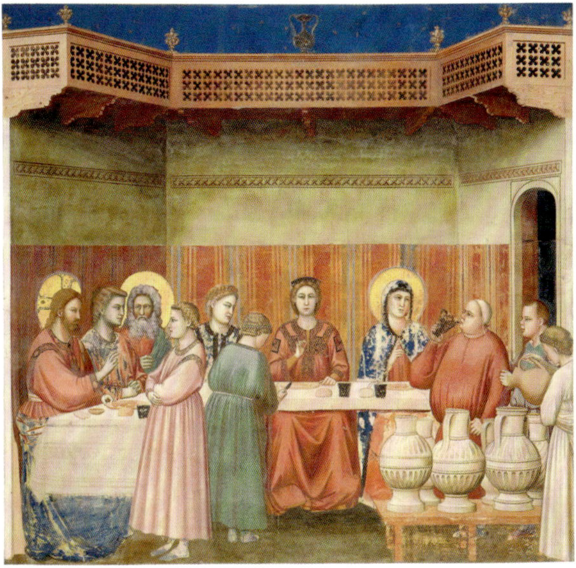

XXIII
The Marriage in Cana

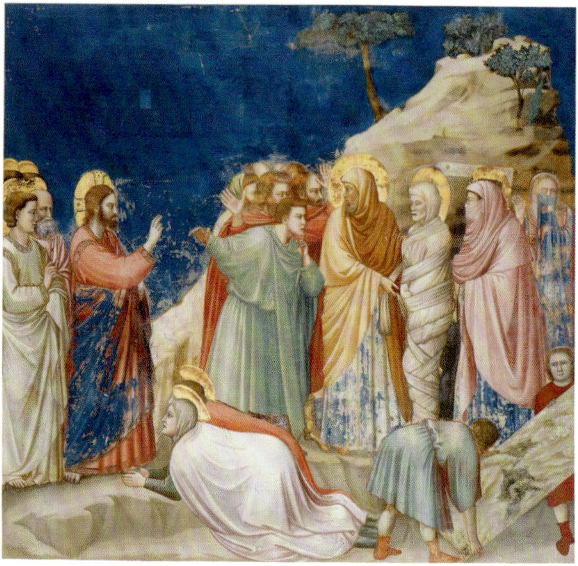

XXIV
The Raising of Lazarus

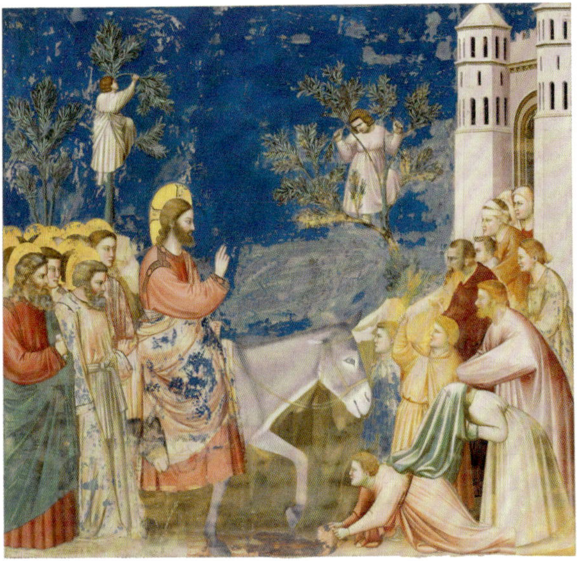

XXV

The Entry into Jerusalem

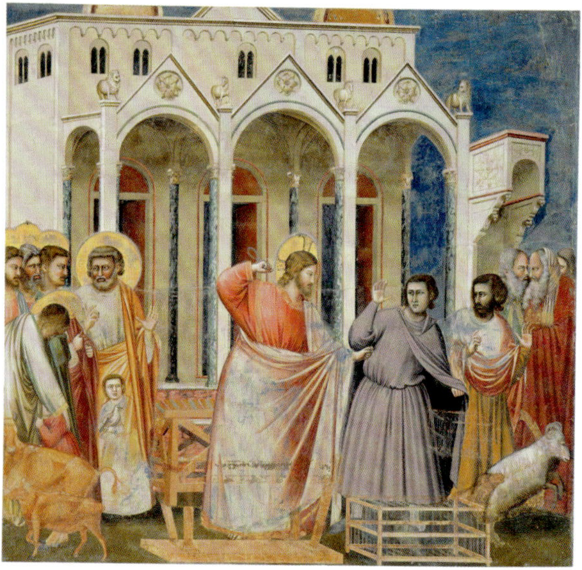

XXVI

The Expulsion from the Temple

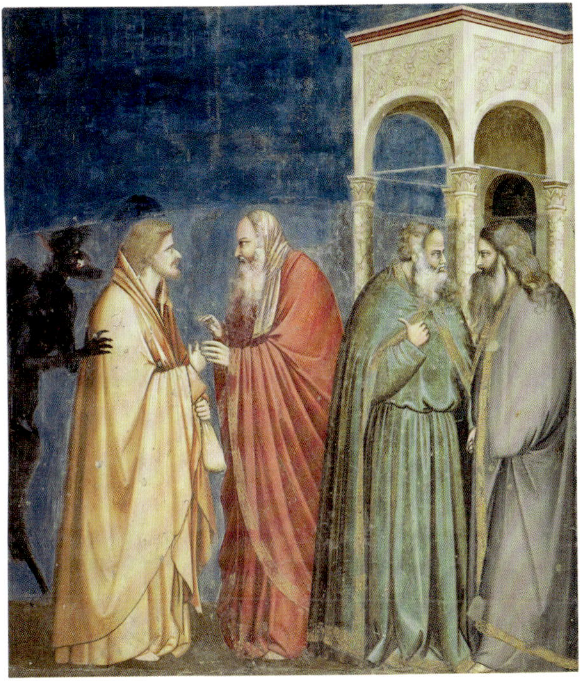

XXVII
The Hiring of Judas

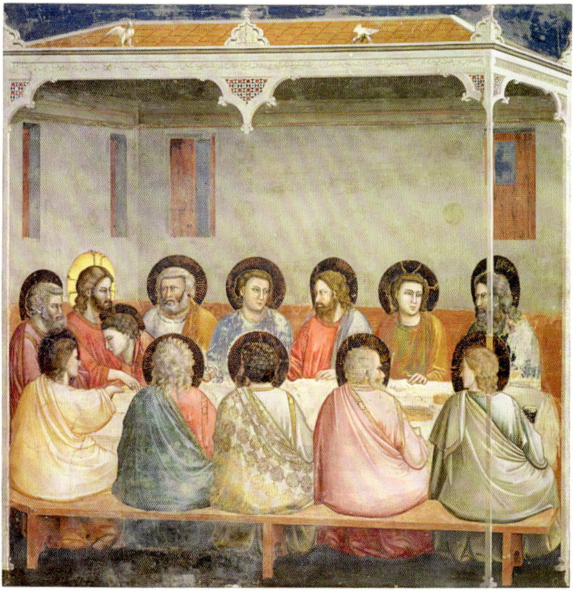

XXVIII
The Last Supper

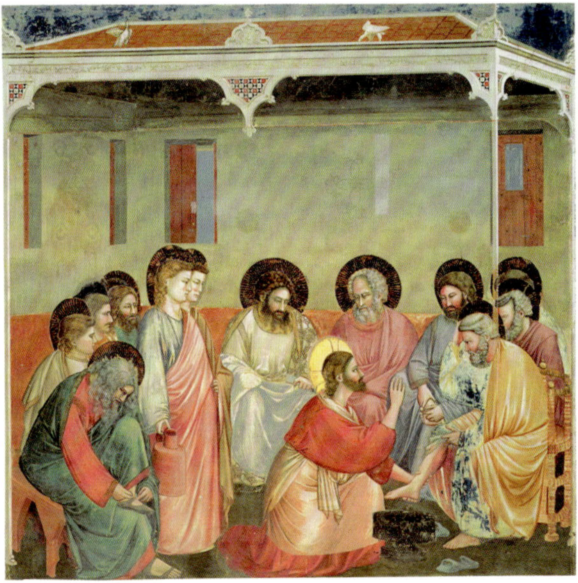

XXIX

The Washing of the Feet

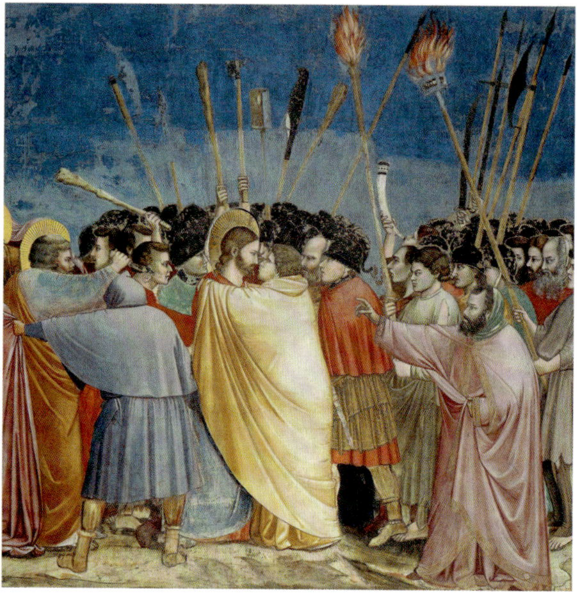

XXX
The Kiss of Judas

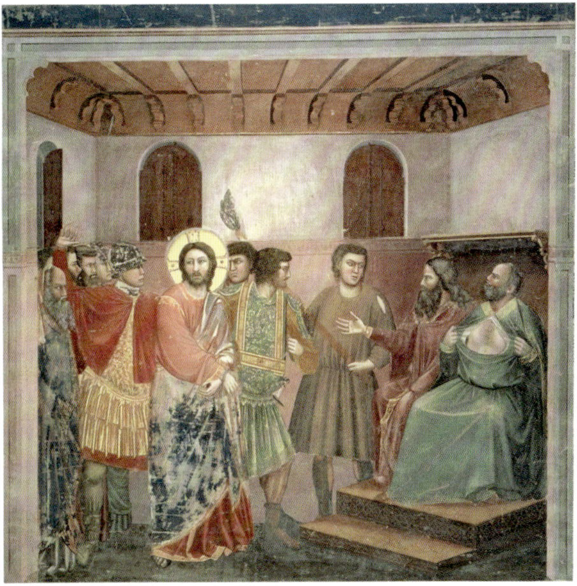

XXXI
Christ Before Caiaphas

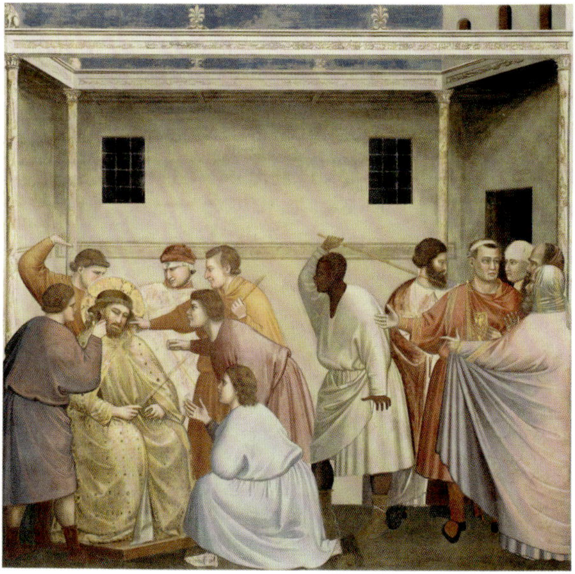

XXXII

The Scourging of Christ

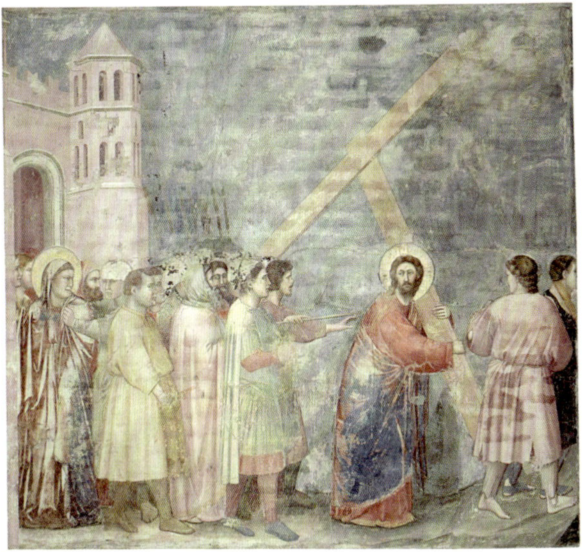

XXXIII
Christ Bearing His Cross

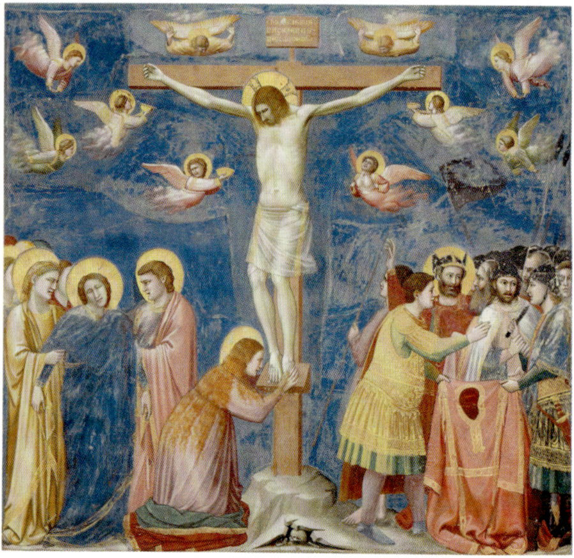

XXXIV
The Crucifixion

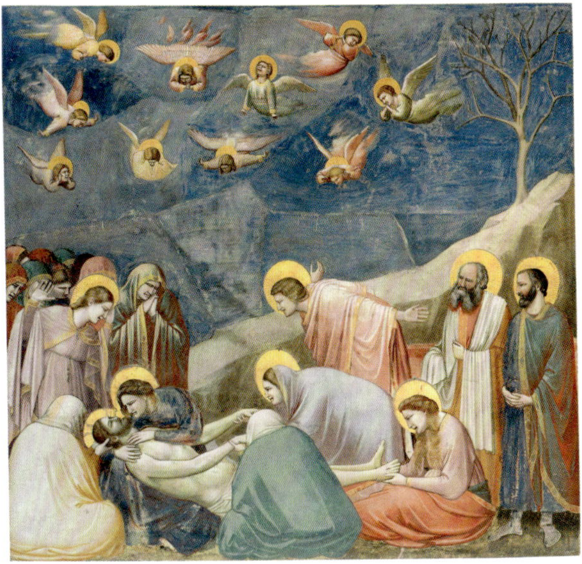

XXXV

The Entombment

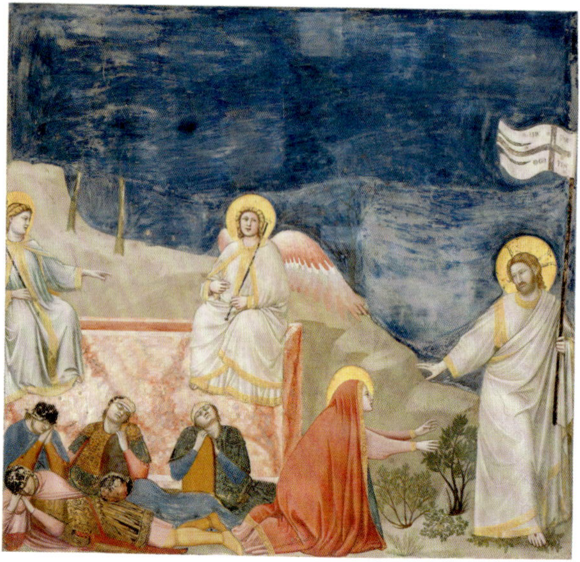

XXXVI

The Resurrection

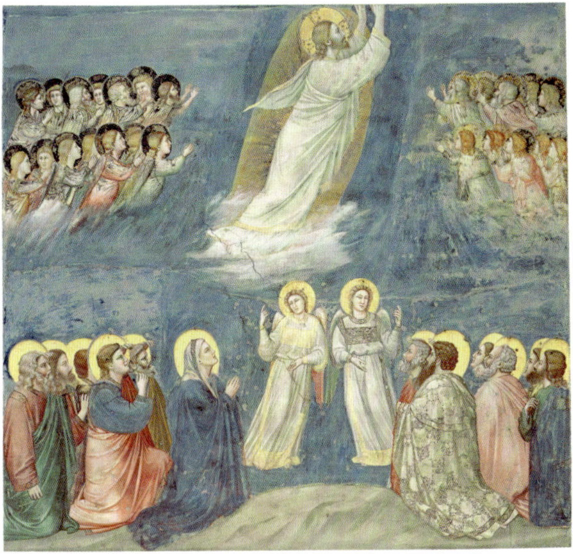

XXXVII
The Ascension

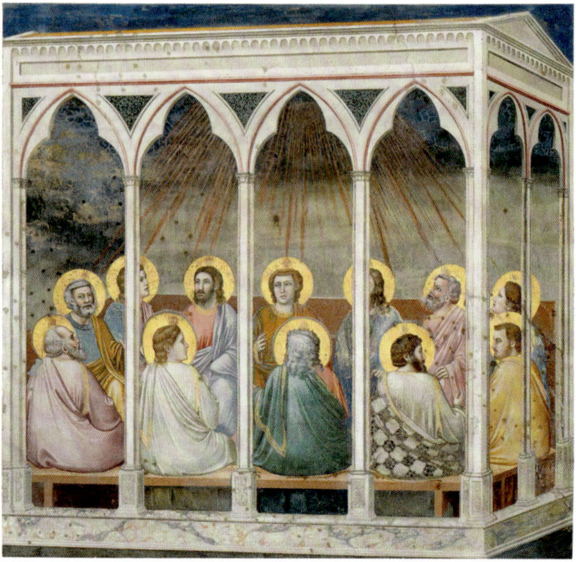

XXXVIII

The Descent of the Holy Spirit

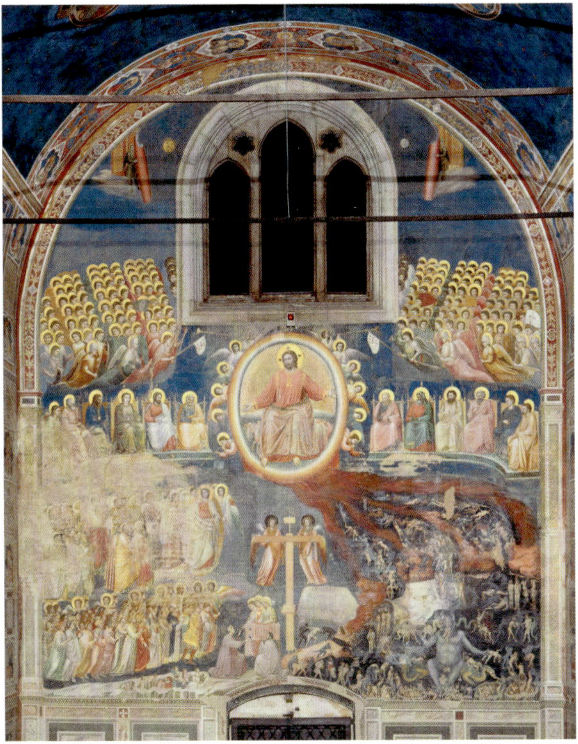

The Last Judgment

[Ed. note, 2018: Ruskin does not discuss this final panel in his text, but it is an important part of Giotto's fresco cycle and is included here for the sake of completeness.]

JOHN RUSKIN (1819–1900) was an English critic of art, architecture, and society, who sought change through his polemical prose. Best known for his five-volume treatise on art, *Modern Painters*—published volume by volume from 1843 to 1860—Ruskin applied Romantic thought to art criticism, rather than relying solely on religious tradition. In doing so, he opened up possibilities surrounding the appreciation and understanding of art, through emotive descriptions, rather than illustration. Particularly intrigued by the painting of the Gothic Middle Ages, Ruskin felt that painters such as Giotto and Fra Angelico were the ideal subject for modern painters. Ruskin's then novel insistence that art and architecture are the direct expression of the conditions in which they were made, continues to influence the study of these fields today.

GIOTTO (c. 1267–1337) is widely known for his role in liberating Italian painting from the Byzantine style of the early Middle Ages. Mainly active in Florence, although he may have been trained in Rome, he also worked in Avignon, Padua and Naples (1328–1332). His contribution to painting was acknowledged by Dante, his contemporary, and later by Vasari. His style is associated with a supreme sense of the momentous and his individualized, emotive figures are depicted with three-dimensionality while inhabiting plausible architectural spaces. Besides the Scrovegni Chapel, Giotto's main surviving fresco cycles are those in the Bardi Chapel and Peruzzi Chapel in Santa Croce, Florence, probably painted before 1328.

ROBERT HEWISON is a British cultural historian who has combined a life-long study of John Ruskin with an active engagement in contemporary culture. He became interested in Ruskin when he wrote a television adaptation of the Whistler v. Ruskin libel trial, and returned to Oxford to take a research degree that led to his first book, *John Ruskin: The Argument of the Eye* (1976). In 1978 he curated *Ruskin and Venice* at the J.B. Speed Art Museum, Louisville. He has edited two collections of essays on Ruskin, *New Approaches to Ruskin* (1981, reprinted 2015) and *Ruskin's Artists: Studies in the Victorian Visual Economy* (2000). In 2000 he co-curated *Ruskin, Turner and the Pre-Raphaelites* at Tate Britain and in 2009 published *Ruskin on Venice: "The Paradise of Cities."* In addition to a career as an arts journalist and broadcaster, he has held chairs at Lancaster University and City University London, and was Slade Professor of Fine Art at the University of Oxford in 2000. In 2017 he delivered a course on Ruskin for the Graduate School of Architecture, Planning and Preservation at Columbia University, New York.

"Ekphrasis" is traditionally defined as the literary representation of a work of visual art. One of the oldest forms of writing, its meaning originated in ancient Greece, where it referred to the practice and skill of describing people, objects, and experiences through vivid, highly detailed accounts. Today, ekphrasis is more openly interpreted as one art form, whether it be writing, visual art, music, or film, being used to define and describe another art form in order to bring to the audience the experiential and visceral impact of the subject.

By bringing back into print important but overlooked books—often pieces by established artists and authors—and by commissioning emerging writers, philosophers, and artists to write freely on visual culture, David Zwirner Books aims to encourage a richer conversation between the worlds of literary and visual art. With an emphasis on writing that isn't academic in the traditional sense, but compelling as prose, and more concerned with subject matter than historical reference, *ekphrasis* invites a broader and more varied audience to participate in discussions about the arts. Particularly now, as visual art becomes an increasingly important cultural touchstone, creating a series that encourages us to make meaning of what we see has become more compelling than ever. Books in the *ekphrasis* series remind us, with refreshing energy, why so many people have dedicated their lives to art.

OTHER TITLES IN THE *EKPHRASIS* SERIES

Ramblings of a Wannabe Painter
Paul Gauguin

Pissing Figures 1280–2014
Jean-Claude Lebensztejn

The Psychology of an Art Writer
Vernon Lee

Degas and His Model
Alice Michel

Summoning Pearl Harbor
Alexander Nemerov

Chardin and Rembrandt
Marcel Proust

Letters to a Young Painter
Rainer Maria Rilke

FORTHCOMING IN 2018

On Contemporary Art
César Aira

Duchamp's Last Day
Donald Shambroom

Giotto and His Works in Padua
John Ruskin

Published by
David Zwirner Books
529 West 20th Street, 2nd Floor
New York, New York 10011
+ 1 212 727 2070
davidzwirnerbooks.com

Editor: Lucas Zwirner
Copyeditor: Clare Fentress
Project Assistant: Mary Huber
Proofreader: Dorothy Feaver

Design: Michael Dyer / Remake
Production Manager: Jules Thomson
Printing: VeronaLibri, Verona

Typeface: Arnhem
Paper: Holmen Book Cream, 80 gsm; GardaMatt, 130 gsm

Distributed in the United States and Canada by
ARTBOOK | D.A.P.
75 Broad Street, Suite 630
New York, New York 10004
artbook.com

Distributed outside the United States and Canada by
Thames & Hudson, Ltd.
181A High Holborn
London WC1V 7QX
thamesandhudson.com

ISBN 978-1-941701-79-9
LCCN 2017960019

Photography Credits

Frontispiece, p. 7:
Photo: Ashmolean Museum, University of Oxford

pp. 14, 59, 106:
Photos: The New York Public Library

pp. 165, 173:
Photos: Alinari / Bridgeman Images, New York

pp. 138, 139, 141, 142, 143, 144, 145, 148, 149, 155, 156, 158, 163, 164, 167, 169:
Photos: Bridgeman Images, New York

pp. 137, 147, 153, 159, 160, 161, 162, 170, 171, 172, 174, 175:
Photos: Cameraphoto Arte Venezia / Bridgeman Images, New York

pp. 140, 152, 154, 166:
Photos: De Agostini Picture Library / A. Dagli Orti / Bridgeman Images, New York

pp. 146, 150, 151, 157, 168:
Photos: Mondadori Portfolio / Archivio Antonio Quattrone / Antonio Quattrone / Bridgeman Images, New York

David Zwirner Books

ekphrasis